In Season, Out of Season

'Preach the word; be instant in season, out of season.'

II Timothy 4.2

Eric James

In Season,
Out of Season

Sermons 1996–1997

SCM PRESS

0 334 02790 X

First published 1999
by SCM Press
9–17 St Albans Place, London N1 0NX

SCM Press is a division of
SCM-Canterbury Press Ltd

Typeset at Regent Typesetting, London
and printed in Great Britain by
Biddles Ltd, Guildford and King's Lynn

For
Stuart Owen
at Ripon College, Cuddesdon,
preparing to preach to the next generation

Contents

Preface

The years covered by this volume – 1996 to 1997 – have been for me years of considerable change. On 31 December 1996, the charity Christian Action closed down after fifty years' work. I had been its Director for sixteen years. On 31 March 1997, I ceased to be Preacher to Gray's Inn. I had been privileged to hold that office for nineteen years. I had reached 'three score years and ten' in 1995. The Psalmist, in Psalm 90, uses those words in a rather sombre and sobering setting: 'The days of our age are threescore years and ten; and though men be so strong that they come to fourscore years; yet is their strength then but labour and sorrow: so soon passeth it away, and we are gone.'

In April 1997 I had a slight stroke, which made it clear that I could not complete the biography of Bishop Trevor Huddleston, on which – it will be clear from some of the sermons within – I had been working for several years.

It is therefore with a thankful heart that I record that in the years 1996 to 1997 I, nevertheless, preached 'in season, out of season', well over a hundred sermons, of which therefore, this volume is but a selection.

I should like to acknowledge the help the staff of SCM Press have been to me in preparing this volume and also Miss Janet Wells.

Eric James

I

Vocation

St Peter's, Vauxhall; 14 January 1996

'Jesus said: "I saw you under the fig tree before Philip spoke to you."'

John 1.48

Vocation is a complex affair.

For instance many years ago – in the 1960s – I had to travel down to Bath, to speak to some clergy. I remember the occasion well, because it was at the time of the publication of Bishop John Robinson's *Honest to God*, and most of the clergy present were against his ideas, and therefore against what I felt I had to say that day.

On the way back, I felt very exhausted by all the opposition, and decided I'd have a meal on the train – they were much cheaper in those days! I was glad to find a table with two seats, both empty, and purposely chose one facing the people coming into the restaurant car, hoping that, seeing my dog-collar, they would want to avoid sitting at my table, and leave me undisturbed. They did – all but one person, who came in when I was half way through the soup.

As soon as he began to sit down, without my ever having spoken to him before, I was overwhelmed by the conviction that I must say to him: 'You'll never be happy till you're ordained.' I struggled for a while against the idea of saying that to a complete stranger, but eventually gave in. So I looked at him, plucked up my courage, and said just that: 'You'll never be happy till you're ordained.' To my astonishment, he replied: 'I know,' and quickly added, 'but, you see, I've just signed on for three years in the Tanganyika Police Force, and am on my way there.' 'Thank God,' I said, 'because if you really *have* a vocation, that'll test it!'

I didn't set eyes on that young man again for many years. But, in 1972, after travelling through half the Anglican Communion, I fetched up in Sri Lanka, and the Bishop of Kurunegala there said to me, when he met me at the airport: 'There's a young priest in my diocese who wants to meet you while you're here. He says you had a great deal to do with his ordination.' The Bishop mentioned his name, which, at first, I didn't recognize. But then my mind went back to that restaurant car in the train from Bath, all those years before. When I actually met that young priest, in Sri Lanka, he had quite a story to tell. He had eventually trained for ordination in Canada. At this moment – in 1996 – he's a priest out in Dubai.

I tell you that story, because, to those who deal with vocation to ordination, that kind of story isn't all that strange. For a while, I used to serve on selection boards for ordination candidates, and I came across several stories like the one I've just told you.

But now I want to say something quite different. I want to say that that isn't the normal or usual way that people discover they have a vocation to ordination. You may remember, in the Acts of the Apostles, that on one occasion, it says, they had a lottery, and the lot fell on Matthias. That's how they chose *him* for the ministry. But again, that isn't the usual and normal way that people discover their vocation – though choosing people for this and that appointment in the Church of England is, often, a bit of a lottery!

I said at the start that vocation is a complex affair.

I said that for a number of reasons. I worked at a riverside wharf on the Thames for seven years during the war, from the age of fourteen until I was twenty-one, and that's where it looked as though I was going to be for life. My brother, four years older than I, is a priest, and was ordained in the early years of the war, and, at first, I assumed that vocation to ordination was for people like him, and not for people like me.

Vocation is a complex word, too. People don't use it for

every job. You don't say someone has a vocation to be head of the Stock Exchange, though I could see someone using all their gifts and doing a great job of service in that position. I heard a woman on the radio this week saying she always felt she had a 'vocation' to be an MP, 'But,' she added, 'people don't seem to want women MPs.' Another person said they had a vocation to be a teacher, but if they were offered a headship now, they'd refuse it.

I think 'vocation' is a very important subject for every human being to consider from time to time, and especially those who 'profess and call themselves Christians'.

Recently, I've come to know an unemployed person in County Durham, who's had a series of jobs. He's struggling to learn how to handle a computer and a word processor. He has a wife and three young children. He drives a taxi, part-time, to get a little money. I wonder what the word 'vocation' should mean in relation to him – and his wife. Or does vocation only relate to the middle and upper classes? My job was to see that that man from a mining community got a word processor of his own, because his gifts need training if they are to develop.

Let's go back to my text from the Gospel for today: 'I saw you under the fig tree before Philip spoke to you.' I wonder what exactly Jesus saw. Was it Nathanael's gifts *then* or his potential? And what precise gifts made Jesus see a vocation in Nathanael?

Nathanael, in the Gospel, is bracketed with Philip. Vocations often, I think, come out of relationships. Such gifts as I have, have depended for their realization on several friends and mentors. You'll remember Nathanael exclaimed: 'Can any good thing come out of Nazareth?' I was born in Dagenham, and someone said to me with a smile only the other day, when they heard where I came from: 'Can any good come out of Dagenham?' Can any good come out of Vauxhall? Is it a place where vocations are being fostered?

You will note that this subject of vocation comes to us in the Gospel for a Sunday after Epiphany, which, you'll all know, means 'manifestation'. Where, I wonder, and how, are the gifts God has given each one of us being manifested? Where we work? In our homes? In our relationships? In the church? In the world at large? Does Jesus only see one or two of us under the fig tree? People who are ordained, or are going to be? Or does he see everyone of us 'under the fig tree'? I believe he does. Do you?

One of my mentors, Eric Abbott, a great friend to me when I was a student at King's College, in the Strand, taught me to say as a prayer:

Thou hast prepared a place for my soul,
prepare my soul for that place.

It's a prayer I've used now for fifty years! It awakens and sustains an awareness in one that each one of us has been seen 'under the fig tree'. And the beauty of it is that you can go on saying it, to your dying day:

Thou hast prepared a place for my soul,
prepare my soul for that place.

2

In Memoriam: Charles Fletcher

Gray's Inn Chapel; 28 January 1996

It's rarely obvious for the Preacher what should be the subject of his sermon on this first Sunday that we meet in Chapel in the New Year. On the Fourth Sunday after the Epiphany, Christmas already seems a long while ago, and the camel train of the Wise Men has long since departed from Platform 1, so to speak.

But I know well what I *want* to preach about this morning. I want to speak about a wise man – one of the wisest men I have known – who died only a few days before Christmas. He was full of years, eighty-four of them, but his death, and funeral the Friday before Christmas, coloured, certainly, my celebration of Christmas this year, and not only mine. Yet, at first, I questioned whether it could be right, in the Chapel of an Inn of Court, to preach a sermon about a doctor, an agnostic doctor, albeit one of the greatest doctors and one of the wisest men of our time. And then, I took courage, and convinced myself that it's not so very odd of me to want to talk to you, my friends, about another of my friends – whom, almost certainly, you will never have met. It's not all that odd, on reflection, to want to share with one's friends the things and people we have loved, from whom we ourselves have received wisdom. So, this morning, let me talk to you, rather than preach, about Charles Montague Fletcher.

In fact, I first met Charles' wife, Lou, who was the daughter of the lady, literally, Lady Mottistone, who ran our old people's club, in Westminster, when I was a curate, nearly fifty years ago. And then, when I first went from Westminster to be chaplain of Trinity College, Cambridge, in 1955, I soon heard of Charles' father, Walter Morley Fletcher, who had been Senior Tutor of Trinity around the outbreak of the First World War. And, later, I read letters of his, when I was writing my book on the eccentric clergyman F. A. Simpson. Simpson had been admitted to Trinity from 'another place' by Fletcher senior in 1911. Charles Fletcher was born only a few months later.

Charles was educated at Eton and Trinity: got a 'First' in both his first and second year exams at Cambridge, and in his third year rowed in the Cambridge boat. He only missed becoming a Fellow of Trinity because his great friend Alan Hodgkin, the Nobel Prize winner, was his chief competitor. Charles was offered a Fellowship at Peterhouse, but his father, who had by then become the first Secretary of the Medical Research Council, suddenly died, and Charles, now twenty-one, decided to do medicine, and to come to London, to St Bartholomew's Hospital, where he would be given a free education in his father's memory.

Charles' father was a man of formidable intellect and energy: a great scientist, a Blue and an FRS; but, I suspect, he was largely responsible for Charles' perpetual inability to value himself, in spite of all his gifts and achievements; so that from time to time he would suffer severe depressions, which, on occasions, only shock treatment could relieve. I learnt at Trinity that, quite often, brilliant dons, however kind they were as parents, unconsciously set standards for their children which they found very threatening.

It was in the last of his Cambridge years that an incident occurred which Charles in later years never tired of describing, and to which I never tired of listening. He went with Alan Hodgkin to a meeting of the Physiological Society in Cambridge which was addressed by Lord Adrian, the future OM and Master of Trinity. Adrian demonstrated that day how the rhythmic electrical activity could be recorded from the surface of the human head. Charles conveyed to me – forty year later – the huge significance of Adrian's work, so that I, who knew little or no physiology, was caught up in the excitement of that occasion, and felt that I myself had been allowed into one of the great moments of scientific and medical history: indeed, of human history. Charles had a wonderful capacity to communicate.

His first job, as Nuffield Research Fellow at the Radcliffe Infirmary, Oxford, coincided with the outbreak of the Second World War. It was at this time that he developed the diabetes that would be with him for life. While he was at Oxford he was chosen to be the very first person to give an injection of penicillin to a patient. Five days after the injection, the improvement of the patient was astonishing.

In November 1942, having returned to Bart's, Charles and Lou were married. In 1945, they went off to Cardiff, where Charles had been put in charge of the research unit for the miners' disease, pneumoconiosis, by the Medical Research Council.

There was always passion and compassion in Charles when he talked of the social consequences of illness and unemployment. But for him, neither passion nor compassion were enough. In his work in South Wales, for instance, he fulfilled Blake's words: 'He who would do good to another must do it in minute particulars.' But the 'minute particulars' in Charles' life were often of considerable significance to others.

He was acutely aware, particularly amongst the miners of South Wales, that he was Eton and Trinity, and that the circumstances of his patients' upbringing had been very different from his. Characteristically, he decided personally to photograph every one of the miners who were his patients at Llandough Hospital. It was a marvellous way of bridging social barriers and getting to know each individual. Rather pleased with the photograph of one of his patients, Charles asked him: 'What do you think of it?' 'Not bad, *considering*,' the patient enigmatically replied. 'Considering what?' asked Charles. 'Considering the photographer,' replied the patient, to Charles' delight.

In 1952 Charles returned to London, to the Hammersmith

Hospital, as Reader in Clinical Epidemiology. There he pursued his studies among London postmen that would eventually result in his work *The Natural History of Chronic Bronchitis and Emphysema*. It was in 1952 that, at the unusually young age of forty-one, he was made a CBE. Charles was a member of the Socialist Medical Association and a vigorous supporter of the National Health Service.

Worried about smoking, he persuaded the Royal College of Physicians to set up a working party, with him as its secretary. Their report rapidly sold out, and Charles played a major part in the formation of the pressure group Action on Smoking and Health: ASH. As late as 1995 he contributed to a symposium with the somewhat ironic as well as menacing title *Ashes to Ashes*. The fact that last year only 28% of men smoked, compared with 52% in 1972, is due, not least, to Charles' labours. There's no doubt it was life-saving work.

Charles' time at Hammersmith was his least happy time. He developed tuberculosis, but, laid up for a while, he found himself reflecting on the failure of many doctors to explain to their patients the nature of their illness and its treatment. In 1973 he produced a small but valuable book, *Communication in Medicine,* and he extended his work to television – not without fierce opposition from many of his colleagues – and became the presenter of the programme *Your Life in Their Hands*. His handsome features seemed even to improve with age, and he became something of a television star.

In fact, I first met Charles rather late in his life, at a gathering of Trinity men and their wives, in about 1973. There is, of course, no surprise in that. A dozen or so years before, I had been chaplain of Trinity. The surprise is that that particular gathering was by way of being a religious retreat; and I had been reliably informed that Charles was an agnostic, and that his agnosticism needed to be respected. Well, Charles was hardly more agnostic than I; but, from the first, I admired and respected his utter integrity. He was certainly a humanist, and the dictum of Terence, *Homo sum: Humani nil a me alienum puto*, could have come straight from not only Charles' lips but from his life. Nothing human was alien to him.

Late the first evening of that retreat, Charles came to me, and, with great and characteristic courtesy, asked whether he might receive the holy communion next morning. He explained that he was an agnostic and knew he would never be able to find a form of words, a credal affirmation, that would enable him to be numbered among the 'paid-up' Christians, so to speak; but to refrain from stretching out his hands to receive the sacrament, would itself, he said, be a kind of negative credal statement from which he equally recoiled.

I was, I remember, deeply moved when, in the chapel the next morning, I placed the sacrament into Charles' outstretched hands. That afternoon, we walked and talked over Blackheath: the first of many such talks on, literally matters of life and death, for in 1989 he became a member of the Working Party on Prolonging Life and Assisting Death, set up by the Institute of Medical Ethics.

It's obvious to you that I am not a medicine man. Charles would have said that he was as obviously not a priest. But I would beg to differ. Charles, I would say, was a born priest: an interpreter; a go-between; a prophet, with the courage a prophet needs; a man in the midst – which is what a priest has to be. Charles was a priest both *to* his profession and *for* it – not least through his part in *Your Life in Their Hands*. In our age, the complexity of medicine, the huge escalation of both its bureaucracy and its technology, call for someone who by his interpretative humanity can proclaim that the heart of the medical profession is still the same: is still essentially and inalienably personal. Charles, all his days, was a medicine man, giving due weight to both those words; but, as I have said, more even than a medicine man. He was a priest, by the way he used his skill and science. His knowledge was never intimidating, always healing.

It was for me a great delight that, in retirement, Charles and Lou came to live in Lambeth, in West Square, not far from where I also live.

I remember encountering Charles one Palm Sunday, a few years ago, at the Festival Hall, at the Bach Choir's performance of the St Matthew Passion. With all his agnosticism, which I must not minimize, I remember reflecting that Charles was treating the occasion like an Act of Devotion on a pilgrimage. And there was no doubt, not only in my mind, when he died, that the chorale 'Be near me, Lord, when dying' should paradoxically be at the very centre of his funeral.

Our last talks together were after Charles had suffered several strokes, and his speech was gravely impaired. One afternoon, when he was nearing the end of the road, I took him some plain chocolate, which I knew, as a diabetic, he loved. He insisted that he himself open the package, which he had to struggle with: it was so securely sealed. The task was all but beyond him, but he resisted any attempt on my part to help him. When, eventually, he broke open the package, there was a look of triumph in his eye, and he offered me a piece of chocolate, with his frail hands, as though he were now the priest and I the communicant. I said to him: 'Charles: the sacrament!' and his face lit up with a seraphic smile. It was not many days later that I was privileged to give him the Blessing for the last time, and to say, with Lou alongside: 'Go forth upon thy journey . . .'

Charles went on ahead that evening, to explore what we all, in the not far distant future, must also explore. And there's no one I'd more want to hear, describing what he has already been excited to discover of that Undiscover'd Country. I like to think of him as one of the Wise Men of our generation, travelling still, and encouraging us all to travel towards the Epiphany.

3

The End of Work

Gray's Inn Chapel; 11 February 1996

'And about the eleventh hour he went out, and found others stand-
ing idle, and saith unto them, "Why stand ye here all the day idle?"
They say unto him, "Because no man hath hired us."'
Matthew 20.6–7

The powerful but peculiar parable of the Labourers in the
Vineyard has always been poignant for me, ever since I
worked, over fifty years ago, at a riverside wharf on the
Thames. Before the National Dock Labour Board Scheme was
brought in, early in the Second World War, men would stand
around in crowds at particular places, like the dock entrance,
anxiously waiting for others to come and hire them. It was
often a question of the survival of the fittest – and the
youngest. The bronchial and the tubercular, the arthritic, the
asthmatic and the aged were likely to be ignored or, at least,
left till last. The boss's agents got to know the labourers who
could move most goods in a day, whatever they were. That
ancient bibilical scene was as modern as could be conceived, in
1939.

But, in more recent years, this parable has been present to
my mind as I have been privileged to journey from one scene
of unemployment to another, meeting this unemployed individual and that. But now it's not only the aged and the ill who
hang about idle. It's the late teenagers, and the young and
virile, who, in a place like, say, Peterlee, in County Durham –
and in thousands of other places – have never had a job since
they left school.

It has recently been reckoned that global unemployment

has now reached its highest level since the great Depression of the 1930s. More than 800,000,000 human beings are now unemployed, or grossly underemployed; and that figure is likely to rise sharply between now and the turn of the century, as millions of young aspirants for work find themselves without a job, many of them victims of a technological revolution that has fast replaced, and is still replacing, human beings with machines, in virtually every sector of the global economy. Last year, in a single month, in the USA, their largest employers laid off 108,000 workers.

Undeniably, we are entering a new phase of world history, in which fewer and fewer workers will be needed to produce the goods and services the global population needs or requires. One American economist, Jeremy Rifkin, has recently written a compelling and disturbing book called simply but baldly *The End of Work*. It examines the various technological innovations and the forces that are moving us to, comparatively speaking, a worker-less world. He explores the promise and the peril of this Third Industrial Revolution, and attempts to address some of the problems that are bound to accompany the transition into such an era.

'But,' you may say, 'your text comes not from a social and economic history, ancient or modern, but from a parable.'

True. But I do not myself think I am wrong to hear the age-old anxiety about employment *within* this parable. Neither do I believe I am wrong to find it, for that very reason, the bearer of a powerful message to our era, already dominated, and increasingly dominated, by the problem of unemployment. And, what's more, I believe that for our age it is 'the eleventh hour'.

It is sometimes helpful and instructive to look away from our own scene in order, paradoxically, to see it the more clearly. In 1949, Rifkin reminds us, only 6% of the cotton in the South of the USA was harvested mechanically; by 1964 it was 78%. Eight years later, 100% of the cotton was picked by machine.

The push of mechanization in Southern agriculture com-

bined with the pull of promised work and wages in the industrial cities of the North to create in the United States one of the
largest mass migrations of history. Between 1940 and 1970,
more than 5,000,000 black men, women and children migrated north, in search of work. By the time that migration
was over, more than half of the black Americans had moved
from South to North, and from an entrenched rural way of
life, to become, at least potentially, an urban industrial prole-
tariat. By 1964, blacks were experiencing an unemployment
rate of 12.4%, while white unemployment was only 5.9%. As
one civil rights activist quipped, 'It's as if racism, having
put the Negro in his economic place, stepped aside to watch
technology destroy that place.'

After the riots in Watts, in 1965, which spread to Detroit
and other Northern industrial cities of the USA, one of the
local residents said: 'The whites think they can just bottle
people up in an area like Watts, and then forget about them.'
Martin Luther King, from his prison cell in Birmingham,
Alabama, lamented the ever-worsening self-image of black
Americans, who were 'forever fighting a degenerating sense of
"nobody-ness"'.

I speak about the experience of the United States, not least
because there is a dramatic clarity about their situation; but I
have myself little doubt that the technological revolution in
Great Britain – and the effect of the global revolution on
Britain – has a great way yet to run, and any underestimation
of that revolution *here* can only lead to an underestimation of
the concomitant social revolution there is bound to be for
millions.

Perhaps the most serious fact is that by the late 1980s, one
out of every four young Afro-American males in the USA was
either in prison or on probation. In the nation's capital,
Washington DC, 42% of the black male population between
eighteen and twenty-five years of age are now either in gaol, or
on parole, awaiting trial or being sought by the police.

In *Newsweek,* in 1994, there was this articulate cry from a
prisoner serving a sixteen-year sentence for murder:

We, the imprisoned, are America's shame. The real crime here is that of your folly. Millions of people in this land languish wasted, under-achieving . . . Society has no use for them outside, so it pays to lock them out of sight, without opportunity or spiritual rehabilitation. But watch out . . . our numbers are enlarging, our costs are rising swiftly. Building bigger and better . . . prisons does not begin to confront the reasons behind the problems and the madness.

It is, to my mind, folly to attempt, as some politicians have done, to dissociate crime and unemployment, or to pretend that it is not the cause of much crime.

I recommend you a book, *Children and Crime,* by Professor Bob Holman. He grew up during the Second World War, but was evacuated from his East London home eight times, his family being bombed out twice. His early experience had a profound effect on him, and led him to train as a child welfare officer. Later, he entered academic life, and became Professor of Social Administration at Bath University; but, concerned about the remoteness of academics, he moved to a large council estate, Easterhouse, in Glasgow, to continue being alongside the disadvantaged.

Holman quotes the economist Will Hutton as saying: 'Unemployment is the single most important cause of poverty, and plays a key role in provoking family breakdown, social distress and the growth of criminality.'

Holman himself gives three ways in which crime is connected with unemployment. First, he says, unemployed young people can become so desperate that they steal to survive. Secondly, he says, unemployment can entail a boredom and futility that lead to delinquency; and that boredom and futility connect, of course, with the drug culture, and drugs are costly, and so lead to other forms of crime. Thirdly, he says, in a society which still tends to value men through their jobs and occupations, the man who cannot make his mark through his work is tempted to make it by vandalism and mindless violence.

I would myself add a fourth connection between crime and unemployment. I believe that in our age, in our market economy, the huge power of advertising presses people, almost irresistibly, to possess what only the purchasing power gained through employment can enable us legitimately to possess. Of course, that means that crime comes from greed and envy; but often that greed is for fairly ordinary and reasonable possessions on the part of the poverty-stricken. This greed is hugely stimulated, encouraged, enticed, and excited by the advertising industry. Advertising plays upon the criminal potentialities of the unemployed. It offers, so to speak, food and drink to starving people. What is available becomes an all but irresistible compulsion. I believe the scale and nature of advertising today is near criminal. It is a major incitement to criminality, and as such shares some of the guilt of the criminal. And over against the poverty of the unemployed there is the seemingly undeserved affluence – often the hugely disproportionate affluence – of many of the employed, who have achieved employment often by that same luck of the draw which has brought others to unemployment; for unemployment is most often due to forces beyond the control of the unemployed. And it simply will not do to dismiss the situation with defensive and glib phrases such as 'the politics of envy'.

Every member of our society has a right to participate in its production, its products and its benefits: not least the benefits of the technological revolution 'Why stand ye here all the day idle?' They say unto him: 'Because no man hath hired us.' What more could they say? What more can most of the unemployed say today?

I believe that reflecting on the parable of the Labourers in the Vineyard may help us all to confront afresh these profound problems, as the crime rate in our cities rapidly rises in just those places where there is most and, most often, long-term unemployment.

As so often in the Gospels, the parable speaks of that prophetic reversal when 'the first shall be last, and the last, first': which reversal there has to be if our world is to be set right. The technological revolution has to be matched by a social revolution. And the sign and sacrament of that revolution in the parable – which is a parable of 'the Kingdom' – is that simple but strange phrase: 'they received every man a penny'.

In the Kingdom, everyone receives the same. Everyone receives that which enables him to know himself to be valued and valuable, equally valued and valuable, no longer thrown on society's slag heap. And enough is enough. To be valued and valuable, to the unemployed, is, indeed, more than enough.

But how do you convey to each man and woman now unemployed – or who will be, in the outworking of the technological revolution – in Liverpool, Gateshead, Newcastle, Manchester, London, Hastings, wherever, this sense of value and dignity, at this eleventh hour? The escalating crime rate, as I say, warns us, at this point, of the urgency of the question.

Jeremy Rifkin highlights the fact that most governments in the West have sought at least to buy time by developing training and re-training programmes; but part of his book is a call for people and governments to move beyond what he calls 'the delusion of training for non-existent jobs'. In a world that is phasing out mass employment, he says that when anyone speaks glibly of the importance of training and re-training you should force them to be specific, and to answer the question 'Training for *what*?'

Given that there will still be some formal work for some, Rifkin insists that that formal work will need to be shared out much more than it is now, which will mean shorter hours and more leisure for many. But the question of what can motivate that sharing, Rifkin sees as of huge importance; and many of you who now lead busy lives and work long hours will understand well enough that it's not easy to see the way towards that job-sharing without a considerable escalation in costs, even if the sharing of the kind of job you do is conceivable.

Much of Rifkin's courageous, and, to my mind, prophetic book concerns the encouraging of what he calls 'Work in the Third Sector', which he sees as the only realistic alternative to a massive increase in police protection and the building of more prisons, to incarcerate a growing criminal class of the unemployed.

Rifkin's 'Third Sector' consists of those who will be involved in community activities: from the social services to health care; education; research; the arts; religion; leisure; organizations to assist the elderly, the disabled, the mentally ill, and the educationally disadvantaged; the homeless, and those who care for the environment. These activities are not to be thought of as luxuries. There's a lot of necessary work, like nursing, which cannot and should never be computerized.

Of course, this 'Third Sector' of Community Service will also require financing, and that finance can only come from those who are already in formal work; so, too, will training for this 'Third Sector' require financing. The alternatives – as Rifkin realistically recognizes – are more police and more prisons to deal with the insurrection of the unemployed. The financing of this 'Third Sector' I myself see as stemming from and implied by that symbolically suggestive phrase in the parable, to which I've already referred: 'They received every man a penny': an appropriate social wage in return for real and necessary work on behalf of society.

It is not for me, in a single sermon, to spell out in detail what Rifkin outlines in his book. It is not even for me to attempt to persuade you of his solutions to the problems of society as he outlines them. It is simply for me to press the question: 'Is there much doubt of Rifkin's perception: that we are entering a new phase in history, characterized by the steady but inevitable decline of jobs as we have known them?' and to ask, 'Given such a future of inevitable and inescapable decline in work and jobs, are there better alternatives than those Rifkin suggests? If so, what?' Rifkin suggests, to make people know themselves valued and valuable, not simply by the provision of welfare in a welfare state and society, we have to build strong local communities that can withstand all the forces of technological displacement.

What I have suggested to you this morning is that the Parable of the Labourers in the Vineyard has much that is relevant, pertinent and profound to say to us at this 'eleventh hour'. I do not myself believe it will 'do' to imagine that any of the present political parties have yet seen clearly enough the future shape of society that lies inescapably only just ahead, or to think they are prepared with solutions, not even *'New Labour'*. And I believe Christians in our country – and not only Christians – have to be people of vision, renewed vision, at this time, not least for the sake of those, young as well as old, who stand, even now, and have stood, many of them, for years; and will stand, for many more, all the day idle.

4

A Southwark Farewell

*Christ Church, Blackfriars; Address at the
Retirement of Peter Challen as Senior Chaplain
of the South London Industrial Mission,
24 February 1996*

I feel very privileged to be allowed to take some part in this tribute to the ministry of Peter, which is both 'Hail' and 'Farewell' to him: 'Hail' to all that he has done since 1967, and 'Farewell' at the end of a remarkable ministry.

I speak to you as someone who, thirty years ago, in 1966, plotted with John Robinson, then Bishop of Woolwich, Peter's appointment. I think there were then five or six overt ingredients to his appointment.

The first was, primarily, John Robinson's knowledge of Peter as an undergraduate at Clare College, Cambridge, where John had been Dean from 1951 to 1959; though, by 1966, I too, knew Peter a little.

The second ingredient was Peter's ministry in Sheffield, in Goole and in Dalton, which included all the years since Peter had been ordained, in 1958, and which meant that Peter was known, appreciated, valued and loved by that great and pioneering Bishop of Sheffield, Leslie Hunter. When I said one day to Bishop Hunter, 'What do you do on your day off?' he said, 'I go to Goole'! Leslie Hunter had been Bishop of Sheffield for twenty years before Peter was ordained, and had appointed, in 1944, as part of his pioneering, the unique Ted Wickham to be Diocesan Missioner to Industry in the Sheffield. Incidently, I myself went on a course on Sheffield Industry, run by Ted Wickham, when I was a theological student. Another young chap on the course was someone called Ronnie Bowlby!, later Bishop of Southwark.

When John Robinson and I discussed the possible appointment of Peter from Sheffield to Southwark, I remember we talked in the gallery of the Convocation of Canterbury that was meeting in Church House, Westminster. The significance of that gallery meeting was that we were where we wouldn't be seen by Peter, who was himself by then a young Proctor in Convocation for the Diocese of Sheffield.

The third ingredient was SLIM, the South London Industrial Mission, which had been pioneered by Canon Colin Cuttell from 1948 to 1963, at the behest of, and in the shadow of, Cuthbert Bardsley when Provost of Southwark, later Bishop of Coventry. (Cuthbert Bardsley came up into the organ loft of Southwark Cathedral when I was playing the organ one lunchtime, just after his appointment, and said, 'I've been praying that God would send me some people to help wake up this Cathedral. I think you may be one . . . Could you meet me in the Harvard Chapel this evening?'!) Colin Cuttell had come to Southwark in 1945, and his work was strengthened and confirmed by Robert Gibson, who was, significantly, called Senior Chaplain of SLIM, from 1962 to 1967. So Peter entered into something which had already had a good deal of pioneering on its behalf. There was already a team. One has only to mention, for instance, the unique ministry of Cecilia Goodenough within this team.

The fourth overt ingredient of Peter's appointment was what was already being popularly called 'South Bank Religion'. Bishop Mervyn Stockwood had come to Southwark in 1959. Without him, John Robinson would never have been appointed Bishop. Others of us had also been in Southwark seven or eight years when Peter was invited here to be rector of Christ Church, and to head up the Industrial Mission. My job at that time, as a Residentiary Canon of Southwark, was to fulfil the brief Mervyn Stockwood had given me: to do all I could to forward the mission of the church in the riverside areas of the diocese, and to see that the church in the suburban

and rural areas of the diocese understood the riverside situation. Peter's appointment was, to both Mervyn and to John
Robinson and, indeed, to me, a significant strategical appointment on the South Bank.

The fifth overt ingredient was the tradition of chaplaincy in
the Church of England, complementary to parish priesthood.
Peter was being asked to take on the small but not insignifi-
cant parish of Christ Church, Blackfriars, which I had known
well when, as a layman, I worked at Emerson Wharf, on
Bankside, the site where the new Globe Theatre is now arising.
But the parish of Christ Church and its church were to be used
(I choose the word 'used' carefully) with the huge and indispensable help of Marshall's Charity as the base for the South
London Industrial Mission chaplaincy. And chaplaincy in the
Church of England was the first recognition, with nevertheless
a surprisingly long history, that the territorial, residential
world is not the only world to be served and penetrated by the
gospel and the church. The phrase 'the plural society' was
becoming popular in 1966: a recognition that society had
many sectors, and that each sector needed to be served and
penetrated by the church, not only the domestic and residential. The logic which had led to hospital chaplains, prison
chaplains, chaplains to the Forces – like 'Woodbine Willie' in
the First World War – was being followed in the appointment
of industrial chaplains.

However, what was clear then was that chaplaincy was too
often attached to 'personalities' and too little to theology. A
brilliant personality, like Cuthbert Bardsley, might make and
leave his mark on, say, Siemens Works, Woolwich; but very
few at that time were asking penetrating questions about, say,
the arms trade that Siemens conducted or, indeed, about the
relation between workers and bosses there. Chaplaincy then
was primarily about chaplaincy to certain sorts of people.
What industrial chaplaincy needed was men and women of
theological as well as pastoral insight.

In Peter we did not receive an academic theologian but we
did receive a theologian: someone who would never cease to

ask penetrating theological questions, not least at the London Business School. Peter rightly calls himself a 'jobbing theologian'. And he did not only ask questions about work on the riverside areas of the diocese, he asked them about the work of all who worked in and from the diocese. And no one has ever questioned Peter's utter integrity.

Peter did more even than ask questions about people's work. He asked questions about people's identity in relation to the world of work. That is to say, he was unwilling to accept the world's facile definitions of people's identity such as 'redundant'. In a world in which much work as we had known it was disappearing, he made it clear that what both work and the lack of it do to people's identity was within his remit. And, because the lack of work could be as destructive as having some kinds of jobs, we learnt that 'the world was Peter's parish': the world with its global economy. Peter has pressed global theological questions.

Peter has never denied that there is romance to industrial chaplaincy, but he made it clear it was not something to be romantic about. It was something to be realistic about – about, for instance, questions of accountability.

There are a number of important aspects of industrial chaplaincy which I shall not be able to deal with, in this deliberately brief address. I would have liked to have spent some time underscoring the fact that Industrial Mission is essentially and inalienably ecumenical.

I would have liked to have spent some time on the question of finance and Industrial Mission. Anglican arrogance so often gets its account – and its accounts – of the finance of Industrial Mission wrong; but it also clearly reveals – has revealed – how little it cares for Industrial Mission by what is does, or fails to do, about financing it.

I would have liked to have spent time on Industrial Mission and the theology of ministry, not least because one of the happiest times I have ever spent with Peter and with John Robinson was at the Roman Catholic seminary for Worker Priests at Pontigny in France, to which, by coincidence,

Thomas à Becket was also glad to escape, a little earlier. At Pontigny, at the generous invitation of Cardinal Lienart, Bishop John Robinson celebrated Mass for everyone there – but everyone: Catholic Worker Priests as well as our largely Anglican delegation.

When one of the Worker Priests at Pontigny, Daniel Chopin, came to Southwark to make a reciprocal visit, he asked me to 'explain' to him factory chaplains. I stumbled as I made the attempt, and Père Chopin's Fernandel-shaped face took on a very uncomfortable appearance. Eventually, in broken English, Daniel Chopin exclaimed: 'If I 'ad a factory chapolin come to the bench where I work, I would say to 'im "Tourist! Sightseer! Scram!"' Perhaps that anecdote should now be filed in the annals of Industrial Mission and Ecumenicity.

I would have liked to have spent time on what I will simply call 'staying there'. (I actually proposed that the Archbishop's Commission on Urban Priority Areas should be called the 'Staying There' Commission.) It is to my mind important that Peter has stayed here, with SLIM, twenty-nine years. ('Thirty years among us dwelling,' wrote Thomas Aquinas!)

But I have purposely left till last the sixth ingredient in Peter's appointment, which I simply label 'Family'. It so happens that I knew Peter's father when I was a boy. He was a nearby vicar in what was known as London-over-the-Border, on the north bank of the Thames. Even in the 1940s Peter's father was ecumenical and open in a remarkable way. He had been a curate to Leslie Hunter at Barking, Essex – to the same Leslie Hunter who, as bishop, would ordain Peter to Sheffield. So Peter came to us here shaped by his father and his family; and the influence on them of Leslie Hunter was comparable with what it was on Peter.

But then, under 'family', I must also, of course, make mention of Ruth. I do not know a more gracious, or more profound wife than Ruth. What Peter would have done without his wife and family I just do not know; and, what's more, neither does he. But I know that I couldn't fail to mention

Ruth – and mention her most honourably today – whom Peter met when she was working for Mollie Batten at William Temple College. I could not fail to include her in the 'package' we received when twenty-nine years ago Peter was appointed to SLIM. And how well he has done! And how well we have done in having him! and how much we shall miss him – and Ruth. And how we wish them well in all that lies ahead.

5

In Memoriam:
Canon Douglas Rhymes

Southwark Cathedral; 16 March 1996

'Mercy and truth are met together.'
Psalm 85.10

There was a superb and sparkling sketch in the Royal
Shakespeare's *Shakespeare Revue,* which ran for many
months at the Vaudeville Theatre last year. An ambassador,
who's been absent from Elsinore for three years, returns, and
casually asks: 'And how's Hamlet?' 'Hamlet?' one of the
gentlemen at court replies. 'Hamlet is dead.' The ambassador
is shocked and appalled. 'And Laertes?' he asks. 'He's dead,
too.' 'And the fair Ophelia?' 'Dead.' 'And her father,
Polonius?' 'Dead, as well. And Gertrude. And Claudius. And
Osric. And Fortinbras. And Horatio, Marcellus, Bernardo,
Reynaldo, Francisco – all dead.' 'O grievous anecdote,' says
the ambassador, somewhat prosily.' To *be* is *not* to be.'
    When I asked myself why Douglas should have asked me to
preach at his memorial service, I soon found myself thinking
of him, seated one day at his desk, drawing up his will, and
saying to himself: 'Now who was at Southwark – at the
Cathedral – in my day?' And having to confront the truth,
much as that ambassador did at Elsinore: 'Stockwood: dead.
Robinson: dead. Gilpin: dead. Southcott: dead. Stanley Evans:
dead. Pearce-Higgins: dead. Tasker: dead. Gordon Davies:
dead.' But then, with relief, he says, 'Ah! There's Eric . . . he's
not *quite* dead – yet.'
    But as I dwelt on that scene, the humour began to dis-

appear, as I watched the idea commend itself to the Douglas we all knew and loved. You see I was, for many years, Douglas' confessor, and I could well see the Douglas who loved both mercy and truth characteristically wanting the person who knew him, not least through the confessional, to preach at his memorial service. But there are, of course, reasons why that won't quite do. The lips of a confessor are sealed, even when the penitent has gone to his grave; indeed, his lips are sealed more than those of others. And as to his judgment of the person; getting to know someone in the confessional, over a period of years, has always seemed to me to teach one how complex and convoluted are the springs of both virtue and vice. Mercy and truth need to meet together. But what *is* truth?

However, I have thought, it may be Douglas chose me to preach today more as your representative than as his confessor, as the one to try to meet the undoubted need of his friends: our need of saying simply what Douglas meant to us. And I shall try to do just that.

I have, in fact, tried to do it in my choice of text, because I believe that mercy and truth *were* met together in Douglas with a combined force, in compassionate concern and concern for truth. When, for instance, you read his writings: *No New Morality, Prayer in the Secular City*, and his recent, more autobiographical *Time Past to Time Future*, you are left in no doubt of that. But his writings did but articulate and focus his life. There was no gap between his writings and his life.

I don't suppose there are many of us here today who remember Douglas, fifty years ago, as an army chaplain. In fact, some of his later friends, I know, found the very idea of Douglas as a tanks chaplain, in the Westminster Dragoons, almost too difficult to entertain and envisage. But in his autobiography there's a passage which not only lets us into the secret of those particular days, for Douglas, but into, one might almost say, the secret of his ministry. He writes:

I found this period in many ways the most satisfying of my whole ministry – for three reasons.

First, I have never been so identified with those whom I have served as I was in the army. I was living the same life and sharing the same dangers and feelings in a way which has never been true in civilian life. Normally one of the difficulties of being a clergyman is that you sense a great gap between your life and that of most of your parishioners. In that situation the stereotype given you emphasizes the gap, but it was not so in the army . . . I saw my work as much more pastoral than official, and was treated accordingly . . .

Secondly, my army service taught me how much could be achieved if one got alongside people, how little if one did not. I found this to be true also of my fellow officers – the more they demanded that they should be treated as superior the less they received respect . . .

Thirdly, I learnt that what is called 'folk religion' is never to be despised. There are many levels of approach to the spiritual and some are far more instinctive than reasoned. In the army, where fear of the unpredictable is closely linked with anxiety about what is happening to relationships at home, but where there is a strong sense of community with one's fellows rarely experienced in civilian life, there will be many mixed motives and reasons for coming to worship or to prayer or discussion with the padre which would never take place in civilian life. If one can learn to accept people where they are rather than where we want them to be, much valuable help and teaching can be given which may well have results in later life.

I suggest that mercy and truth were meeting together then and there in Douglas the pastor, at that beginning of his ministry; and they would never be separated throughout all the years of his ministry.

I didn't myself meet Douglas until he came to Southwark, and to the cathedral here, in 1946. By then, his fleeting affair with communism was over. So, too, were his curacies in the

Chelmsford diocese, and, of course, his tanks chaplaincy. But, in fact, my brother John, who is four years older than I, was a priest in the Chelmsford diocese alongside Douglas and has two memories of him, both of which, though very different are, I think, of considerable significance.

My brother had to share a room with Douglas, on a clergy course, just after Douglas had been demobbed. He remembers how Douglas had terrible nightmares, as a result of his appalling war-time experiences – he was one of the first, for instance, to enter Belsen – and remembers how Douglas' unbearable distress woke him in the middle of the night, when he then had to try and calm and comfort Douglas.

His second memory of Douglas is quite different. My brother had to take some candidates to a confirmation at the Chelmsford mission-church where Douglas was then curate-in-charge: the Church of the Ascension. It was a place of little architectural merit, which Douglas was wont to describe as 'a tin tabernacle of the corrugated iron period of Anglican architecture'. When the evangelical Bishop of Chelmsford, Henry Wilson, entered the church, he looked disdainfully at a large open vestment cupboard, displaying several magnificent copes and chasubles, and said, somewhat sarcastically, to Douglas: 'I suppose you would describe those as the cloaks Paul left at Troas.' 'Yes, my Lord,' said Douglas. 'And do you seriously believe,' the bishop continued aggressively, 'that St Paul would have carried garments like that around the Mediterranean basin?' 'Oh no, my Lord,' said the young Douglas, quick as a flash. 'I expect he would have had an excellent portable set like the one we have here at the Ascension.'

Douglas revealed his potential as a parish priest in the Dickensian area that still existed after the war around the cathedral here. And then came his eight years at Eltham, and his election to the Convocation of Canterbury. That was when and where he came to the notice of John Robinson, Bishop of Woolwich.

Douglas was quintessentially a 1960s man. The debate about God was sparked off in 1962 by *Soundings*, a collection of essays Alec Vidler edited to mark the fiftieth anniversary of the publication of *Foundations*. Then came *Honest to God*; but Douglas' *No New Morality*, in 1964, probably did more to provoke people in the Church of England to re-think the church's attitude to sex than any other book. Douglas undoubtedly had a great gift not of original thinking but of popularizing, of communicating. He wrote well and simply. The church has always had a particular need of those who could interpret the scholars and vulgarize their work, in the sense of speaking plainly, in the vernacular, in the common tongue, without debasing or coarsening. Douglas undoubtedly had that gift in abundance.

It was primarily John Robinson who spotted Douglas' gifts, and persuaded Bishop Mervyn to make him a Residentiary Canon and Director of Lay Training, based on Wychcroft, Bletchingley, where with Cecilia Goodenough, in a surprising partnership, they exercised together a remarkable and complementary ministry.

It is perhaps appropriate for me to say at this point that I well remember in 1967 first taking into my hands a copy of Douglas' *Prayer in the Secular City*. I remember particularly how moved I was by its dedication. It simply said: 'To the eight Junior Clergy of the Southwark Diocese who have helped me greatly in my thinking: John Austin, Christopher Brown, Norman Davies, Martin Hughes, Paul Jobson, David Lambourne, Roger Royle and David Wilson.' That was typical of Douglas. You would often find him in the middle of a group like that: talking with them, and listening, and learning; exchanging enthusiastically; wrestling, as often as not, with some matter of mercy or of truth – with laity and clergy, young and old, men and women. He was often a man in the midst. That was an important aspect of what priesthood meant to Douglas.

After six years at Bletchingley, Douglas returned to parochial ministry, to eight arduous years at Camberwell, followed by another eight at Woldingham. And here, I know the many curates Douglas had at Eltham, at Camberwell, and at

Woldingham would all want to pay personal tribute to the pastoral care that he lavished on them in their training. Douglas the pastor was also, in all these situations, Douglas the prophet, characterized both by pastoral diligence and courage, that courage which is called for alike by both mercy and truth.

From that particular assertion I can conveniently go on to say that no memorializing of Douglas would be complete or, indeed, adequate, which did not make mention of Douglas' unique contribution to what I will call the 'Debate about Homosexuality'. And he did that not least as a trustee of the Institute for the Study of Christianity and Sexuality.

And this I *will* say as Douglas' confessor. In my experience, Douglas was concerned every year – and to the end – to go on growing, spiritually and personally. This distinguished him from many, both homosexual and heterosexual. And lest any should imagine Douglas to have been in any way blindly homosexual, let me read you a single paragraph from his autobiography, which, I believe, speaks volumes.

> The so-called 'gay' world is often no more understanding and compassionate than the 'straight' world. 'Gay' clubs and pubs are not places where real friendship and love may be found but rather 'pick-up' contact points for one-night stands: if the face or the age does not fit, the person will be ignored and so will experience an even greater sense of loneliness and exclusion than he or she would in a more general place of relaxation. As a result, the same kind of negative unreality is found in the very world that is loud in its protest against the attitudes of heterosexual society – the unreality of assessment not by character or personality but by genital activity. It is strangely ironic that society, church and the 'gay' world itself are all obsessed with the purely physical: what is done in bed becomes far more important, in terms of approval or disapproval, than creative human relationship.

It must have taken considerable courage for Douglas to write that paragraph, in 1992, when he was by then nearly eighty years young.

May I just say that I hope that any of his friends who have not yet read Douglas' *Time Past to Time Future* will read it, in thankfulness for his life. In his last years Douglas was prone to the depression that particularly afflicts the aged: when it seems, from time to time, that nobody wants us any more and that our work is done. I well remember, in one of our sessions together, suggesting one day to Douglas that he should work at some kind of autobiography. I suggested it, frankly, to keep him occupied. I had no idea that what he wrote, nearing eighty, would result in such a very creditable book. As Bishop Simon Phipps wrote in his Foreword: 'This is a book of clear integrity, coming, as it does, from one who has lived out, in sustained action, the implications of what he has come to believe.'

Those who teach others about preaching are wont to advise them to avoid the word 'finally' at the end of a sermon. But I think there may be a context and an occasion when that rule should be broken, and that is when one is talking of the death of someone in, say, a memorial sermon like this.

Finally, Douglas had to face his own death. How he wanted to do that is foreshadowed in what he wrote, thirty years earlier, in *Prayer in the Secular City,* for he provides the text of a service for Good Friday 1967, in Clapham. The first part he called 'Facing Life and its Meaning'; the second, 'Facing Death and its Meaning'. I found it very moving to read that second section again recently, just after Douglas' death. Those of you who were able to be at his funeral service, and heard Simon Evans' marvellous sermon, will have a fairly clear idea how Douglas in fact faced up to the cancer that brought his life to an end. You will know it was with courage, and you will know that Douglas was ready to die and that he died in peace.

We were told at his funeral that only days before he died, in St Wilfred's Hospice, he was reflecting on those lines from Eliot's *Little Gidding*:

What we call the beginning is often the end
And to make an end is to make a beginning
The end is where we start from . . .

With the drawing of this Love and the voice of this Calling
We shall not cease from exploration . . .

Douglas, of all people, will not have ceased from exploration.
He will have explored, by now, more of that mercy and truth
revealed in Christ, the mercy of the divine Truth and the truth
of the divine Mercy. And one thing is certain. Douglas would
want to say to his friends at his memorial service, 'Do not you
cease from exploration. Let us go on together until the vision
of the divine Mercy and Truth is vouchsafed to us in its full-
ness, and we see him as he is.'

6

The Dunblane Tragedy

Stowe School; 17 March 1996

None of us will have been able to ignore, or, indeed, to forget, the tragedy that occurred at Dunblane Primary School last Wednesday. When anyone does such a deed, we are all bewildered, and are lost for words. Yet, when we have said that the best response is silence, most of us go on to give vent to our confusion in a spate of words, some of them appropriate and necessary words of sympathy for those who have suffered. And it is, I think, understandable that we should want to give voice to our feelings, for a number of reasons: not least because, although the tragedy happened at Dunblane, there are many ways in which we are ourselves deeply and inescapably involved.

The deed was done in Dunblane, but it could have happened anywhere. A very similar event did happen in Hungerford, not so long ago. And, of course, such an event raises so many questions – so many important and insoluble questions:

about God;
about evil;
about human freedom and human responsibility;
about the nature of sanity and insanity and the relation of
    insanity and responsibility;
about forgiveness;
about the sort of society which produces such a person as
    Thomas Hamilton, who did the deed;
about the effects of family background and breakdown;
about violence – not least on television;

and about the use of guns.
And so on. And so on. And so on.

But a sermon is never simply about abstract questions; nor is it only about other people. It should always be relevant to ourselves. How then should we relate this ghastly event profitably to ourselves?

After mulling over that question for some time, I came to the conclusion that it might be right for me to read you a kind of poem which I wrote not long ago. I called it *Making your Mark*. Here it is:

Lord, I think you've made us
so that each of us needs to make our mark.
And if we can't –
or feel we can't –
that only makes us feel we need to make it
all the more.

The more we feel we haven't made our mark,
the more we try to make it:
with extravagant language;
extravagant deeds;
extravagant dress;
extravagant haircuts and cosmetics;
extravagant houses;
and 'big deals':
all trying to prove
we've made it.

Vandalism – wrong as it is –
is often people trying to make their mark,
who feel unable to make it
any other way.
And there are very different kinds of vandal:
and different kinds of mark.

A 'don't care' society – national or local –
that doesn't care whether people make their mark –
will be made to care.

And people who say:
'I've made my mark:
You could have made yours, if only you'd tried'
will be made to care
profoundly.

Some people never feel they've sexually
made their mark;
and make a smash-and-grab raid
on that kind of achievement:
either in fantasy, or actuality, or both.

Some people find
drugs give them
the illusion for the
moment of making their mark.

Some people from their first days
have felt they never could make their mark,
since mother never showed they'd made their mark with
    her,
and she'd never made her mark of care on them.

Some people need a gang
to help them make their mark,
and never could make it alone.
(Sometimes a gang's more blandly called a 'club'
– with tie and reunion dinner.
Sometime a gang is called a 'Party'.)

Some people make it in a teenage gang,
and then, for the first time,
meet someone for whom they're 'everything'

with whom they've made their mark;
and, 'at a stroke', the gang life,
and all the teenage delinquency,
disappears.

Politicians
are often like little children,
striving to make their mark;
and so are rich tycoons.
'Even if I can't,
my yacht will make my mark,
or my Mercedes.'

And some there be
who're so afraid to make their mark,
they stay concealed
within the pin-stripes of conformity.

Perfect love casts out fear
of never making our mark.

But no love, Lord, except Yours,
is ever perfect;
and Your love is never perfectly received,
or understood.

So here I am –
and here are all of us –
always fearful,
to some degree,
of not making our mark:
at a party,
in our school, or in our job –
or in our lack of job.
With the opposite sex,
(and the same one),

and . . .
with You.

So, something of the vandal remains,
always,
in me:
the man who makes his mark
by different kinds of violence.

Kings do it;
terrorists do it;
policemen do it;
broadcasters and journalists do it;
prison governors, warders, and prisoners do it;
judges do it;
clowns and clergy do it.

We were all made to make our mark –
and, somehow, miss it:
or make too large a mark –
for fear of being too small.

Lord, there's something of the vandal in us all.

Whatever happened at Dunblane, whatever the cause of it,
one thing is clear: the perpetrator of that ghastly deed felt he
could make his mark with guns in a way he hadn't been able
to make it by other methods. That is at least part of the
tragedy: the terrible tragedy.

Perhaps that event, besides involving us with sympathy for
those who were bereaved by it, should at least make us ask
ourselves:

How do I make my mark?
How was I meant to?

7

Sacrifice and Service

King's College Chaplaincy; 27 March 1996

The Introductory Sentence appointed for today – from St Paul's Second Epistle to the Corinthians, chapter 5, verse 15 – says that 'Jesus died so that we should no longer live for ourselves but for him who died and was raised to life for us.'

Just before Holy Week, and ten days before Good Friday, it's appropriate that we should hear again that message in all its clarity and simplicity: 'we should no longer live for ourselves but for him who died and was raised to life for us'.

John, in his Gospel, and in his best known words, says much the same: 'Greater love hath no man than this, that a man lay down his life for his friends.' And John implies that Jesus had been doing just that from the first days of his ministry until that Last Supper and those last days, culminating in Good Friday.

And in the next verse John further involves us, just as Paul had done. He tells us Jesus said, 'Ye are my friends if ye do whatsoever I command you' – which is, of course, what a servant does. We, too, are to lay down our lives, but if we do he will no longer call us his servants but his friends. A lot of people, of course, talk a lot these days about 'servanthood' and 'the servant ministry', but as soon as they get an order – which is what servants get – they cry off.

We are to obey his commands, and live no longer for ourselves. We are to lay down our lives. When I was ordained, forty-five years ago, I was taught to say the words 'I will go unto the altar of God . . .' whenever I celebrated the communion; but I was also taught to make it the very first prayer of every day, and to remind myself that whoever I was meeting that day, that meeting itself would be the altar of God: an opportunity for laying down my life for my friends, of no longer living for myself.

Of course, I'd have to confess that I've failed to say that prayer more times than I care to confess. And I must confess that with some people, and some situations, I have found it impossibly hard to think that meeting this particular person and dealing with this particular situation is going to the altar of God and an opportunity for laying down my life as Jesus did. But I've no doubt that that is what it should be. I've no doubt that sacrifice and service should be at the centre of my life and the life of every Christian.

As Holy Week draws near, I'm reminded that when I was a student here at King's, fifty years ago, I spent Holy Week at Mirfield, Yorkshire, with the Community of the Resurrection. The addresses were given by Fr Keble Talbot, the Superior. He said, in one of his addresses: 'At the worst time he did the best deed. The same night he was betrayed he took bread. He used the betrayal as the means of our redemption. That's what redemption's all about,' he said. I've remembered those words all these years. But it was only after twenty-one years that I had to turn the theory into practice, when a particular personal crisis hit me, in 1972, in which I believed, with good reason, that I had been betrayed – within the church – and the question was whether I would allow my life to be embittered or whether I should ask God to enable me to use that betrayal as the means of redemption, my redemption, but not only mine.

If we see our life as one laid down for our friends then as soon as we leave the altar we are on the way to it again: the altar on which we lay down our life for our friends, as Jesus did on Calvary, and as he had been doing hour by hour, in different ways all his ministry.

Whatever our job, as father, mother, solicitor, student, engineer, priest, shop-keeper, doctor, diplomat, in our home and in our job we go to the altar of God. And even if we're out of a job, unemployed, however we fill the hours, there is there and then, opportunity to go to the altar of God and lay down our life for our friends. The situation of the unemployed would, I believe, be transformed if each unemployed person said to himself or herself: 'I may be out of a job, but I'm still God's servant. I'm still in his ministry. And I shall discover who I'm meant to be as I learn to be God's slave.'

In God's service we soon discover that he calls us friends, and that friendship becomes the central relationship of our life. And I'm equally sure that if all employed persons saw their job as the primary place where they can serve God, the world would be a very different place – though I'm aware of the complex and complicated ethical questions that are raised once you see your job as one of the primary places for you to be the servant of God. Almost every job – from arms manufacturing to being a private detective – has its morally ambiguous and compromising situations.

No matter what our place in the world's eyes, and the world's hierarchy, those words of Jesus in today's Gospel can shape our life: 'whoever wants to be first must be the willing slave of all', though Jesus, the servant of God, warns us on the cross and from the cross that there's a price to be paid for being employed in his service; His servanthood cost Jesus everything. We've no reason to think it will cost us less.

Last Sunday, where I was preaching, I found myself talking to a young diplomat, someone in the diplomatic *service*, who wanted to know the implications of Christ's servanthood for him. We are lucky that, in our everyday language, something of this Christian concept, this characteristic theme of service – laying down our life – survives.

It's odd that we have a Prime *Minister*, a first *servant*. It's odd that our government depends on the civil *service*. A week or so ago I had to preach in Southwark Cathedral at the memorial service to Canon Douglas Rhymes. What most people had never realized was that during the war he was a chaplain in the Westminster Dragoons. What they could hardly credit was that he found that period in many ways –

and I quote – 'the most satisfying of my whole ministry' – despite all the horrors of war. He was with some of the first troops to enter Belsen. It occurred to me, as I read what Douglas had written to describe his time as chaplain, that it was significant he could say he was then in 'the Services'.

On Thursday, last week, I had to preach in St Paul's Cathedral at another memorial service, giving thanks for the life of a Professor of Medicine, Charles Fletcher. Charles personified for me much that is best in our Health *Service*. In the Epistle for today we read how Jesus 'offered himself as the perfect sacrifice to God through the eternal Spirit'. In the Gospel for today St Mark tells us 'the Son of Man did not come to be served but to serve'.

If any of us has any doubt where and how we can lay down our life in this world there are literally hundreds of charities which need our service. There are, for instance, 59,000 children in Rwanda who have now no contact whatever with their parents, who may indeed be dead. Save the Children is trying to find their parents. It desperately needs our help.

But I believe we ought to look to our more immediate life as the place of service and sacrifice before we look at charities. It is ten days to Good Friday. It seems to me that at this time God gives us another invitation to renew our consecration as a servant of God. If we want to, this Passiontide can be a real following in the footsteps of Jesus, who laid down his life. 'We are now going up to Jerusalem,' Jesus said. Note that word 'we'. It's an invitation to us, not simply to be servants, but to deepen our friendship with Christ, and with his Father and ours.

'We are now going up to Jerusalem' has almost the same meaning as 'we are going to the altar of God', as we do here and now. At the altar today, this Passiontide, we can renew our commitment, reconsecrate ourselves to the life of service and sacrifice . . . whatever the cost: 'that we should no longer live for ourselves, but for him who died and was raised to life'.

8

St Anselm

It's lovely to be asked to preach at my own parish church. I dislike technical language which is only used by church people; so I dislike the phrase 'patronal festival'. But that's what today is: St Anselm's Patronal Festival, which simply means that this church was named after St Anselm. But some of you will want to know why: why this church, in the middle of Lambeth, was named after St Anselm, and that's not easy to say!

Many people these days are bored if you tell them something happened nearly a thousand years ago. They say, 'That's just history.' And St Anselm is not only 'history', he was born in Italy, which doesn't make him any easier for quite of lot of people to like him – in Lambeth!

So, why do *I* like St Anselm? Well, I like people who can tell a good story, and St Anselm became famous for his stories.

He was a man utterly given to God. He won many a follower by his willingness to discuss any knotty problem. He was a very reasonable sort of fellow, and clearly enjoyed discussing with people their problems of believing. Once, he saw a small boy teasing a captive bird. He didn't go for the boy. He simply said, 'You know: that's just how the devil plays with us,' which I've no doubt made the boy think.

Anselm must rank amongst the finest thinkers and writers of any age, especially the theologians and spiritual writers. In his thinking, he held in balance the absolute justice and the absolute mercy of God.

As a biographer myself, I rather like the fact that when Anselm discovered that one of his monks was writing his biography, he tried to get him to destroy it; but he also treated him kindly and justly.

Anselm was born in Aosta, in northern Italy, in 1033. It was a mountainous area. As a boy, Anselm had a kind of dream or vision. In his dream he thought heaven was at the top of the mountains he could see from where he lived, and felt he was bidden to climb there, and go to the court of God, the great king of heaven. When he got there, God asked him, in a friendly way, who he was, and a servant was told to bring him bread to refresh him. Next day, he told the people where he lived that he had been to heaven, and had been fed by the bread of heaven.

Before he was fifteen, Anselm developed a longing to become a monk. His desire was so strong that he left home, eventually arriving at Bec, in Normandy. There he began to study under the great scholar, Lanfranc. Not until he was twenty-seven did Anselm actually become a monk at Bec.

After three years, he replaced Lanfranc as Prior of Bec. He continued to pursue his reading, his studies and his thinking. He hated the burden of administration he had to carry at Bec, and asked to be relieved of it; but he was told he must stay with it. He wrote nothing for publication for ten years. He was made Abbot of Bec in 1078, when he was forty-five. He was a loving and wise spiritual director to the monks.

The year he was made Abbot, Anselm paid his first visit to England, not least to see his friend Lanfranc, by then Archbishop of Canterbury. It was obvious when Lanfranc died, in 1089, that Anselm should succeed him. Anselm resisted the suggestion with every argument he could muster.

He found the community of monks at Canterbury a haven from the troubles in England between church and state, and church and king – first, William Rufus, and then, Henry I. Between, if you like, Christ and Caesar.

He withdrew a good deal into his study.

He asked the Pope, at one stage, if he could be relieved of

his archbishopric. What was difficult was that there were two popes at the time. Anselm supported one, and the king – and the bishops of England – the other. One of the great friends of Anselm at the time was the Abbot of Westminster. Anselm was seventy-four when he died at Bec, in 1107, on the Wednesday in Holy Week.

Anyone who wants to be a follower of Anselm must be someone to whom prayer is central to their life. The authority of scripture must also be of huge importance. Anselm was a 'man of God' in his life and his thought.

His greatest work was simply called *Why God Became Man (Cur Deus Homo)*. Although this is, of course, about God, it's also about us. It takes human sinfulness very seriously, and that God had to do something about sin and evil. He sent his Son into the world to do that 'something'; but, Anselm is clear, Christ *willingly* underwent the suffering and death that 'something' involved.

Anselm was a great writer; a great thinker; a great theologian; a great man of prayer; a great pastor; and a great archbishop. I know that when Michael Ramsey was Archbishop of Canterbury, and was asked 'Which of your predecessors do you most admire?' he replied, immediately and unhesitatingly, 'St Anselm'. So it doesn't surprise me that a church built so near to Lambeth Palace should be named after St Anselm. I myself feel we are very blessed in having him as our patron.

Let me just end with one of his prayers:

O God, Thou art Life, Wisdom, Truth, Bounty, Blessedness, the Eternal, the only true Good. My God and my Lord, Thou art my hope and my heart's joy.

I confess with thanksgiving, that Thou hast made me in Thine image, that I may direct all my thoughts to Thee, and love Thee.

Lord, make me know Thee aright, that I may more and more love, enjoy, and possess Thee. And since, in the life here below, I cannot fully attain this blessedness, let it at least grow in me day by day, until it all be fulfilled at last in the life to come. Here be the knowledge of Thee increased, and there let it be perfected. Here let my love to Thee grow, and there let it ripen; that my joy being here great in hope, may there in fruition be made perfect. Amen.

9

Dvořák and Easter

Gray's Inn Chapel; 28 April 1996

It's very appropriate, I think, that we should have the Dvořák Mass in D this morning, this Third Sunday after Easter. Dvořák was a devout Catholic; and there's every reason to believe he would have taken Easter very seriously. He wrote his *Requiem* when he was very bereaved by the death of his daughter, his first child.

His music – not least his Mass in D – responds to his world in an intimate, direct and simple way. You can't imagine Easter going by for Dvořák *without* his remembering the death of his daughter. Indeed, you can't imagine him writing a Mass which didn't relate in some way to life and death as he had already experienced it. And he would, no doubt, have hoped that this music would help those who attend Mass to confront the realities of their lives.

I wonder what Easter has meant to you this year – indeed, what it means to you today? I've had two people I've been close to die this Easter. Let me try and say, briefly, this morning, in a simple, direct and intimate way in tune with Dvořák's approach, something of what Easter means to me.

I can't myself believe that life is ultimately without meaning and significance. I can't believe, for instance, that music is just a random collection of sounds; neither can I believe that persons – like Dvořák, and his wife and daughter – and like you and me – are totally random. I don't believe that, in the end, everything is chaos. I believe there is a divinity that shapes our ends.

Even the agnostic A. E. Housman, who died sixty years ago

this week, spoke in a memorable phrase, of lads who 'carry back bright to the coiner the mintage of man'. I believe that the transcendent power of Love is the origin of us all, and will not, in the end, simply throw away and waste who we are. That Love, I believe, has a transcendent purpose for each of us, which we hardly begin to glimpse in the here and now; the Love that created us will gather up the fragments of our lives, and nothing will be lost.

So, although I wouldn't bet my life away on any of the details of the resurrection, I'm not surprised that the transcendent Love which began Jesus' life, and manifested itself within his life, supremely in the cross, should be surprisingly manifested after his life. I believe we're all in for surprises. As my favourite collect puts it:

O God, who hast prepared for them that love thee such good things as pass man's understanding ...

God is the 'God of Surprises'.

Easter, the first Easter, is not only about Jesus, it's about Dvořák, and his daughter, and you and me.

In the last few weeks, I've had a ghastly job to do. I've had to get rid of a thousand books, to make room for a study-cum-office in my home, where, up to now, I've had a guest room. I must admit it's been like tearing half my heart out and throwing it away; but it's had its good side. I've had to look at each book and say 'What does this mean to me now?' In the middle of the mêlée, I came across a leather-bound volume of the funeral service from the Prayer Book, which my uncle, who was a priest in Ottawa for most of his life, left to me. (He also left me his personal prayer book, which revealed that he had prayed for me every day.) Going through that bound copy of the Funeral Service – which had lots of extra prayers and poems pasted into it – I came across this poem by Julia Dorr, about whom I know nothing. It is rather Victorian, but also rather perceptive:

How can I cease to pray for thee? Somewhere
In God's great universe thou art to-day.
Can He not reach thee with His tender care?
Can He not hear me when for thee I pray?
What matters it to Him, Who holds within
The hollow of His hand all world, all space,
Thou that hast done with earthly care and sin?
Somewhere thou livest and hast need of Him.
Somewhere thy soul sees higher heights to climb,
And somewhere still there may be valleys dim
That thou must pass to reach the heights sublime.
Then all the more because thou canst not hear
Poor human words of blessing, will I pray.
Oh! true, brave heart! God bless thee wheresoe'er
In God's great universe thou art to-day.

John Donne was, of course, a much greater poet. Before he
became Dean of St Paul's, he was Divinity Reader at Lincoln's
Inn, so I always feel a special affection for him. On this Sunday
after Easter, when music helps us not only to worship here but
to think of eternal life, one of his verses can well conclude
what I have to say:

Since I am comming to that Holy roome
    Where, with thy Quire of Saints for evermore,
I shall be made thy Musique; As I come
    I tune the Instrument here at the dore,
    And what I must doe then, thinke here before.

10

The Legal Service: Exeter

Exeter Cathedral; 12 May 1996

'Thou shalt show us wonderful things in thy righteousness, O God
of our salvation.'

Psalm 65.5

I have chosen as my text this verse from the Psalms for several
reasons.

First: in Hebrew literature, the idea of righteousness and
the idea of justice are often virtually synonymous. Thus this
verse could well be translated: 'Thou shalt show us wonderful
things in thy *justice* . . .' And that, I suggest, is a highly appropriate thought for such a service as this. The history of our
human concern for justice: local justice; national justice; international justice; justice for the individual; justice for the
minority; justice for the majority, tells us, to my mind, more
about the very nature of our humanity than almost any other
subject.

Secondly: I take a text from a *Psalm,* because I believe this
service should express something even wider than the concern
of Christians in the community; and, great as are the Christian
insights into justice, a verse which emanates from the Jewish
psalter – which was, after all, the prayer book of Christ himself – has much to commend it.

Thirdly: I am, at the moment, drawing to an end my nearly
twenty years as Preacher to Gray's Inn, and I have no hesitation in saying that no book of the Bible has made me think
more on judgment and justice than the Book of Psalms –
judgment, justice and mercy: human and divine, and justice
particularly for the poor. I would have no hesitation in

recommending any Home Secretary to steep himself in the Psalms. On many a court house of our country you will see some words from the Psalms. For instance, 'Defend the poor and fatherless: see that such as are in need and necessity have right' (Psalm 82.3).

There is a fourth, more personal reason why I have chosen this verse from the Psalms. I am engaged at the moment in closing down the charity of which I have been privileged to be the Honorary Director for many years. Frankly, our money, like the money of many charities, has been running out. We are closing down in December, with a service in St Paul's Cathedral, on the fiftieth anniversary of our beginning. The charity, Christian Action, has been concerned all these years for Christian social justice; and, of course, I have found myself looking back at what have had to be our concerns in this past half century. Reflecting thus, I have found myself saying, 'You have shown us wonderful things in your righteousness: in your justice . . .'

Christian Action, in fact, began with a meeting in Oxford Town Hall in 1946. All sorts of political figures gathered there: the young Lord Hailsham, Quintin Hogg; the young Lord Longford, Frank Pakenham; the young man from your locality, Richard Acland; people like Victor Gollancz, and the young Robert Runcie. There had to be an overflow meeting in the University Church. It was one of the first truly ecumenical meetings, with Catholics and Jews on the platform, and Methodists, Presbyterians and Quakers.

Soon, these young radicals, in those post-war months, were energetically organizing an act of international reconciliation. They invited the Berlin Symphony Orchestra to England, with Furtwängler and Celibidache to conduct, and Dame Myra Hess to play a Beethoven piano concerto. They went from London to Huddersfield, to Glasgow and Edinburgh, celebrating reconciliation in and through music.

For fifty years Christian Action has tried each year to ask, 'What injustice is there *now* which we should try to put right?' It has often led to the initiation of another charity, or assisting another charity to survive. You won't be surprised that it has meant being involved in a wide variety of campaigns. To name but a few:

The Campaign for the Abolition of Capital Punishment;
The Christian Action Homeless in Britain Appeal;
The Christian Action Shelter for Vagrant Women;
International Defence and Aid for Southern Africa.

The list could go on. And I'm thankful to be able to record that, after the Brixton riots in 1981, I wrote, as Director of Christian Action, a letter to *The Times* which suggested that the Archbishop of Canterbury should set up a commission on the problems of the inner city, which eventually, he did. Christian Action contributed a considerable amount of its resources to the promotion of the work of that Commission, which resulted not only in the Report *Faith in the City,* in 1985, but in ten years of work, not only in the inner cities themselves, but to make areas of Britain that Bishop David Sheppard calls 'Comfortable Britain' aware of the injustice perpetrated in Britain, not least, but not only, in the urban priority areas of Britain.

Of one thing I am now certain: justice is not something that is secured only in our courts, important as that may be, and, indeed, is. The spiritual resources for the pursuit of justice are of huge importance. They should, of course, be a prime concern of the churches – and not only of the churches.

Sometimes, when considering such a subject as justice, I find it helps to look right away from the scene with which we are most familiar. To read, for instance, such a book as Eberhard Zeller's *The Flame of Freedom,* subtitled *The German Struggle against Hitler* is to read a cautionary tale. How could such a deeply Christian and cultured country be captured by Nazism? It's, of course, easy to say arrogantly, 'It couldn't happen here', but as you read of people like Claus von Stauffenburg, within the Wehrmacht, and, of course, Dietrich Bonhoeffer, within the church, you find yourself profoundly thankful for the struggle for justice that was waged within a web of political and human complexity. 'Thou shalt show us wonderful things in thy righteousness, O God of our salvation' becomes a text that knows no national bounds.

It so happens that less than a fortnight ago, at Gray's Inn, I was privileged to hear the German President, Professor Herzog, who had at one time been the equivalent of our Lord Chief Justice, give a lecture on Constitutional Law. He gave the lecture in the Hall of Gray's Inn, which had been entirely rebuilt since it was razed to the ground in the Blitz. A few yards away from him, as he spoke, was a bust of Winston Churchill and a portrait of Lord Elwyn-Jones, who had served as Counsel for the Prosecution at the Nuremberg Trial. It was impossible to escape reflecting on the nature of reconciliation, and to recall that, though the High Court of Parliament is our supreme court, the authority of the European Court of Justice – since the Second World War – raises, let us say, 'interesting questions'.

I happen to be writing at the moment the biography of Bishop Trevor Huddleston, now a frail and aged man in his eighties. Scarcely a day goes by without my being forced to reflect on some aspect of what I will call 'the South African miracle', embodied in the overthrow of apartheid, with, at its centre, the incredible biography of Nelson Mandela. Christian Action is, I believe, justly proud that before his arrest and twenty-seven years' imprisonment, Mandela slipped out of South Africa and came to England, and called on Canon John Collins, then Director of Christian Action, to plead that we should do all we could both to care for the families of political prisoners in South Africa and also to see that what we knew here as British justice should be made available to those accused in the courts of South Africa. The full story of International Defence and Aid, and the raising of millions of pounds for the purpose, has still to be told; but that my text 'Thou shalt show us wonderful things in thy righteousness: in thy justice . . .' is aptly and appropriately applied to that story there can be no shadow of doubt.

But just as it is sometimes necessary to look away from the familiar scene at home in order to be shown the full scope of the story of righteousness and justice, so it is necessary also to return to the subject of justice and righteousness here at home, lest our attention on what Dickens would have called 'Borioboolagha' be but an evasion of our more immediate responsibilities.

When I preached, recently, at Grendon Underwood prison, I saw there just what could be done with prisoners who want to be helped. Christian Action, in the 1970s, spent much of its time, money and energy, and provided house room, for a new organization entitled Radical Alternatives to Prison. Since those days, in 1981, the Prison Reform Trust has come into existence, for which we have also tried to give some support. One of the many things that have become clear from their work is that community sentences can sharply reduce re-offending, and that much more could be done to unlock the potential of the probation service. Prison sentences are often only a counsel of despair, whereas well-targeted and managed community programmes can reduce re-offending by between 20% and 40%. And to reduce the number of offenders is the best way of reducing those who are victims.

I myself know well what a difference it makes when individuals take time and trouble to relate to offenders, one by one and in small groups. The evidence for the effectiveness of re-habilitative programmes is now sound and substantial, and provides good grounds for all those with responsibility for community penalties. But it is always easier to recommend sentences which put people out of sight and out of mind – not simply of the courts but of the community.

I know of several profitable and promising schemes when and where a few offenders have been carefully allocated to experienced individuals; and I believe it is time now to raise again the flag of 'alternatives to prison'.

You will, I'm sure, have noted what the Archbishop of Canterbury had to say in his Prison Reform Trust Lecture in London only this last week. I myself thought his remarks on prisoners on remand were particularly worthy of note: that they form a fifth of the whole prison population; that the conditions for remand prisoners are some of the worst in the whole prison population; and that remand prisoners accounted for over half of the self-inflicted deaths in prison between 1990 and 1994.

I am, I fear, now old enough to look back to the 1960s, to when I was a vicar of a large inner city parish in South London and, sadly, to have been able to watch and witness nearly forty years of a declining youth service. I believe that a great deal of the personal relationships built in and through the youth service – not, of course, with, in the main, churchgoing youth – were invaluable to society. Over the years, our denying resources to the youth service has been to 'sow the wind', and now we are 'reaping the whirlwind'. In the end, it is personal relationships in society that count. The absence of the personal relationships of creative and imaginary leisure facilities is, to my mind, a major factor leading young people into criminal acts. It's the personal relationships which, above all, help people to know themselves valued and valuable.

Some weeks ago, I was asked to attend, in Gateshead, one of the local hearings of an organization called Church Action on Poverty, and to spend a day with people from the surrounding area, almost all of whom were unemployed. Those who were not unemployed were people like myself, who had been invited to hear what those who were had to say.

It was, I have to say, the unemployed youth, with little or no experience of a job, and little or no prospect of one, who most appalled and distressed me that day. It was as ludicrous to separate the prospect of future crime from present and future youth unemployment – and, indeed, from present boredom – as it was to separate the concept of justice and righteousness from the hard facts of unemployment.

Recently, a book has been published called *Children and Crime*, subtitled 'How can society turn back the tide of delinquency?' The author, Bob Holman, has had a remarkable life. He has left his Chair of Social Administration at the

University of Bath and moved to Europe's largest public housing, Easterhouse, in Glasgow – his wife's home town – to continue to be alongside the disadvantaged in our society.

Future Cabinet Ministers, and probably present ones, should, I believe, go and sit at the feet of Bob Holman, but so should future clergy, magistrates, judges, probation officers, and police. When I read Bob Holman's book I am filled with hope, in a situation which, I know, with reason fills many with despair. Bob Holman, from costly experience, outlines an agenda for us all. And I find myself saying not only 'Thou shalt show us wonderful things in thy righteousness . . .' but 'Thou art showing us – in places like Easterhouse – wonderful things in thy righteousness, O God of our salvation: our health and deliverance.'

In my beginning is my end. I implied, at the beginning of what I've had to say, that the struggle for justice involves us all: parents, police, youth leaders, volunteers, professionals, and so many professions and organizations, so many jobs, so many charities; and that search and struggle for justice, I said, tell us more about the very nature of our humanity than almost any other subject.

That is why I chose to speak to you today on this profound verse from the Psalms: 'Thou shalt show us wonderful things in thy justice, O God of our salvation.'

11

Charles Dickens

Gray's Inn Chapel; 19 May 1996

At the end of one of my first terms as a theological student at King's College, London, the Dean, Eric Abbott, later my great friend, said to me, as he shook hands: 'Think theologically, boy!' He went on to explain that he meant that you have to learn to think theologically whatever confronts you – life, death, sorrow, joy, literature, music . . .

So, this morning, I take as my text Proverbs 14.10: 'The heart knoweth his own bitterness and a stranger doth not intermeddle with his joy.' And I want to think theologically with you about Charles Dickens. I think of Dickens as a person of great interior bitterness, as a very wounded person indeed, but his gifts and his greatness were in some measure the product of his wounds.

In his earliest childhood, before he came to London, Dickens was subject to nervous fits. He was clearly as sensitive as he was sickly. Then, when he came up to London to join his parents, as a boy of nine, he was mortified to find them living in a little garret in one of the poorest streets of Camden Town, and utterly dismayed that their circumstances made them unwilling to continue his schooling. The nervous fits of his childhood recurred. This was but the beginning of troubles. Soon there was the notorious Blacking Factory for him near Hungerford Bridge.

'It is wonderful to me,' Dickens said to Forster, his biographer, 'how I could have been so easily cast away at such an age. It is wonderful to me, that, even after my descent into the poor little drudge I had been since we came to London, no one had compassion on me – a child of singular abilities, quick, eager, delicate, and soon hurt, bodily or mentally – to suggest that something might have been spared, as certainly it might have been, to place me at any common school. Our friends, I take it, were tired out. No one made any sign. My father and mother were quite satisfied. They could hardly have been more so, if I had been twenty years of age, distinguished at grammar-school and going to Cambridge.'

Edgar Johnson, another biographer, comments that this is 'the shock and bitterness of a hurt child that speaks in these words – a child so deeply wounded that the hurt is still there, a quarter of a century later, when they were spoken.' But, only eleven days after the young Dickens entered the Blacking Factory, came his father's arrest and Charles' visits to his father in the debtors' prison, Marshalsea, close by the church of St George the Martyr, Southwark – 'Little Dorrit's Church'.

'No words can express the agony of my soul,' Dickens wrote of his first introduction to the Blacking Factory, 'as I sunk into this companionship; compared these everyday associates with those of my happier childhood; and felt my early hopes of growing up to be a learned distinguished man crushed in my breast. The deep remembrance of the sense I had of being utterly neglected and hopeless; of the shame I felt in my position; of the misery it was to my young heart to believe that, day by day, what I had learned, and thought, and delighted in, and raised my fancy and my emulation up by, was passing away from me, never to be brought back any more; cannot be written. My whole nature was so penetrated with the grief and humiliation of such considerations, that even now, famous and caressed and happy, I often forget in my dreams that I have a dear wife and children; even that I am a man; and wander desolately back to that time of my life.' But he concealed his wounds: 'I never said, to man or boy, how it was that I came to be there, or gave the least indication of being sorry that I was there. That I suffered, in secret, and that I suffered exquisitely, no one ever knew but I.'

Spasms from his old illness recurred again and again, the

body expressing the bitterness of his heart. One such seizure occurred at the warehouse: 'Bob Fagin was very good to me on the occasion of a bad attack of my old disorder. I suffered such excruciating pain that time, that they made a temporary bed of straw in my old recess in the counting-house, and I rolled about on the floor, and Bob filled empty blacking-bottles with hot water, and applied relays of them to my side, half the day. I got better, and quite easy towards evening; but Bob (who was much bigger and older than I) did not like the idea of my going home alone, and took me under his protection. I was too proud to let him know about the prison; and after making several efforts to get rid of him, to all of which Bob Fagin in his goodness was deaf, shook hands with him on the steps of a house near Southwark Bridge, on the Surrey side, making believe that I lived there.'

Charles never forgave his mother for having wanted to keep him working in the warehouse, even after his father had decided to take him out. 'I never afterwards forgot. I never shall forget. I never can forget.'

'The heart knoweth his own bitterness.' The heart of Charles Dickens knew his own bitterness for years after his childhood, indeed, he knew it for life. For years after his time at the Blacking Factory he never had the courage to go near Hungerford Stairs; he could not endure it. There is no shadow of doubt that these years, these traumatic experiences were crucially formative in the life of Charles Dickens.

It is, of course, a commonplace now amongst psychiatrists that the experiences of rejection in early years are likely to shape the whole of a person's future; and there can be little doubt that that is what happened in the case of Dickens. Dickens' son, Sir Henry Dickens, speaks, in his memoir of his father, of his 'heavy moods of deep depression, of intense nervous irritability, when he was silent and oppressed'.

We know that Dickens was the kind of depressive who, after his basic experience of rejection, continually depends on external sources to maintain his self-esteem. A falling off in the popularity of his monthly instalments of his latest novel would plunge him into anxiety and depression. So Sam Weller was played up in *Pickwick Papers* because he was selling well, and Martin Chuzzlewit was sent to America because interest in him was flagging.

We know that Dickens not only turned against himself the hostility within him, born of rejection, hence his recurrent depression, but bent that hostility in turn against others. 'My father was like a madman when my mother left home,' wrote his daughter. 'This affair brought out all that was worst, all that was weakest in him. He did not care a damn what happened to any of us. Nothing could surpass the misery and unhappiness of our home.'

We know that Dickens was the kind of depressive who, to avoid this state of misery, force themselves into activity, deny themselves rest and relaxation, who cannot afford to stop, and may in fact achieve quite a lot that way. We have only to read how *Sketches by Boz* in 1836 was followed by *Pickwick Papers* in 1837, whilst *Oliver Twist* was begun in February 1837, before *Pickwick* was finished; and that *Nicholas Nickleby* followed fast in 1838. And so on. And to follow Dickens walking, and mountain climbing, and putting on plays, and lecturing, and reading in public, is to follow a man possessed, possessed with a devil of ambition, a devil which gave him no rest, but drove him restlessly, relentlessly and sometimes recklessly on in projects of barely concealed self-justification. The rejection of his earlier years must surely have been somewhere near to the heart of all this.

We know that, in those who have experienced rejection, aggression and compassion may occur almost like a see-saw, for they will know from within what it is to be the victim and the under-dog, and they will sometimes explode with hostility, and sometimes over-flow with compassion. The tenderness of Dickens – especially to children – is proverbial. Speaking at a dinner, in 1858, on behalf of the Hospital for Sick Children, he said: 'The spoilt children I must show you are the spoilt children of the poor in this great city . . . for ever and ever irrevocably spoilt out of this breathing life of ours by tens of thousands. The two grim nurses, Poverty and Sickness, who bring these children before you, preside over their births, rock their wretched cradles, nail down their little coffins, pile up the earth about their graves.'

Here tenderness and compassion are combined with aggression, with hostility that has found some relief in a wicked enemy on whom it is justifiable to lavish wrath: the evils of bad housing, slavery, capital punishment, child labour, debtors' prisons – the list of Dickens' 'causes' for which he went to war must be longer than that of almost any other eminent Victorian. He found goal upon goal for the redirection of his hostility, the hostility born of rejection.

And, no doubt in Dickens the actor, Dickens, one might almost say, the *prima donna* – the rather ham actor – who had always to be on the stage, and preferably at the centre of the stage, who was pathetically dependent upon and desirous of crumbs of praise, and as pathetically sensitive to blame; no doubt, here too, are the scars, if not the still open wounds of rejection.

'The heart knoweth his own bitterness – and a stranger doth not intermeddle with his joy.'

The joys of Dickens are interwoven with his bitternesses: that is one reason why we should not intermeddle with them. The rejected Dickens desperately needed the joy of writing and writing and writing, of resolving in imagination what had not been resolved in reality. He as desperately needed the joy of succeeding at the writer's craft, of being accepted in reality. He needed the joy of being centre of the stage. He needed, one may add – with a little of the compassion of Dickens himself for the complexity of human beings – he needed the joy of Ellen Ternan as well as of Catherine. Such terrible rejection had made acceptance by this person and that an insatiable desire; and who are we who have not known his rejection to intermeddle with his joy? Well does Edgar Johnson call his definitive biography of Dickens *Charles Dickens: His Tragedy and Triumph,* for the two are so inseparably interwoven.

But it is possible so closely to relate Dickens' future to his past, his triumph to his tragedy, to relate the creation of his manhood to the psychology of his childhood, that there seems little to him that is not predictable and predestined, like some modern automaton. Whatever else Dickens was, he was not that. There are, I think, three ways of escaping that predicament.

The first is to read something of his humour, though there is almost always pathos in the midst of Dickens' humour, and sometimes even hysteria. The shades of the prison house close in even upon chapters of *Pickwick Papers* . Yet the humour of Pickwick has often something unsullied about it. It seems to have escaped quite free from the world of anxiety and rejection.

Personally, I think that Dickens' humour is never more irresistible than in Mr Pickwick's trial for breach of promise: in Mrs Bardell's drooping entrance and relapse into a state of frantic imbecility, in the entreaties of Messrs Dodson and Fogg, but above all in Sergeant Buzfuz himself:

'The plaintiff, gentlemen,' continued Sergeant Buzfuz, in a soft melancholy voice, 'the plaintiff is a widow; yes, gentlemen, a widow. The late Mr Bardell, after enjoying, for many years, the esteem and confidence of his sovereign, as one of the guardians of his royal revenues, glided almost imperceptibly from the world, to seek elsewhere for that repose and peace which a custom-house can never afford.'

At this pathetic description of the decease of Mr Bardell, who had been knocked on the head with a quart-pot in a public-house cellar, the learned sergeant's voice faltered, and he proceeded with emotion: 'Some time before his death, he had stamped his likeness upon a little boy. With this little boy, the only pledge of her departed exciseman, Mrs Bardell shrunk from the world, and courted the retirement and tranquillity of Goswell Street; and here she placed in her front parlour-window a written placard, bearing the inscription – "Apartments furnished for a single gentleman. Inquire within."'

But, besides Dickens' humour, it is important, secondly, to read alongside descriptions of the social situation of early Victorian Britain some such document as Marx's Manifesto.

Listen to this from *The Working Day* by Karl Marx, from, mark you, the *Daily Telegraph* of 17 January 1860, reporting a meeting held in Nottingham, quoting the chairman, a country magistrate:

> There was an amount of privation and suffering among that portion of the population connected with the lace trade unknown in other parts of the kingdom, indeed, in the civilized world. Children of 9 or 10 years are dragged from their squalid beds at 2,3, or 4 o'clock in the morning, and compelled to work for a bare subsistence until 10,11 or 12 at night, their limbs wearing away, their frames dwindling, their faces whitening, and their humanity absolutely sinking into a stone-like torpor, utterly horrible to contemplate. What can be thought of a town which holds a public meeting to petition that the period of labour shall be diminished to 18 hours a day?

Then, from Reports made in 1860 and 1863 to the Children's Employment Commission:

> J. Murray, 12 years old, says: 'I turn jigger, and run moulds. I come at 6. Sometimes I come at 4. I worked last night till 6 o'clock this morning. I have not been in bed since the night before last. There were 8 or 9 other boys working last night. All but one have come this morning. I get 3/6. I do not get any more for working at night. I worked two nights last week.

And from Law Courts:

> In the beginning of June 1836, the magistrates of Dewsbury, Yorks, were informed that the owners of 8 large mills in the neighbourhood of Batley had infringed the

Factory Acts. Some of the factory owners were accused of having kept at work 5 boys between the ages of 12 and 15 from 6 am on Friday to 4 pm the following Saturday, not allowing them any break except for meals, and one hour for sleep at midnight. These children had to do their 30 hour stretch of work in the shoddy hole, the place in which the woollen rags are torn to pieces, and where the loading of the atmosphere with dust, shreds, and so on, forces even an adult workman to tie a handkerchief over his mouth for the protection of his lungs. The accused worthies, being Quaker, were prevented by religious scruples from taking an oath. They affirmed that, in the tenderness of their hearts, they had allowed a pause of 4 hours in which the poor little children could have slept, but the obstinate youngsters had absolutely refused to go to bed! The Quaker worthies were fined £20.

When you read, for instance, Dickens' description of the boy Jo, from Tom-All-Alone's in *Bleak House,* you then realize that Dickens was not exaggerating. He was appealing to love, pity and shame with all those gifts that had been given him. Listen again, if you will:

It must be a strange state to be like Jo! To shuffle through the streets, unfamiliar with the shapes, and in utter darkness as to the meaning, of those mysterious symbols, so abundant over the shops, and at the corners of streets, and on the doors, and in the windows! To see people read, and to see people write, and to see the postmen deliver letters, and not have the least idea of all that language – to be, to every scrap of it, stone blind and dumb! It must be very puzzling to see the good company going to the churches on Sundays, with their books in their hands, and to think (for perhaps Jo does think, at odd times) what does it all mean, and if it means anything to anybody, how comes it that it means nothing to me? To be hustled, and jostled, and moved on; and really to feel that it would appear to be

perfectly true that I have no business, here, or there, or anywhere, and yet to be perplexed by the consideration that I
am here somehow, too, and everybody overlooked me until
I became the creature that I am! It must be a strange state,
not merely to be told that I am scarcely human (as in the
case of my offering myself for a witness), but to feel it of
my own knowledge all my life! To see the horses, dogs, and
cattle, go by me, and to know that in ignorance I belong to
them, and not to the superior beings in my shape, whose
delicacy I offend! Jo's ideas of a Criminal Trial, or a Judge,
or a Bishop, or a Government, or that inestimable jewel to
him (if he only knew it) the Constitution, should be strange!
His whole material and immaterial life is wonderfully
strange; his death, the strangest thing of all.

Jo comes out of Tom-All-Alone's, meeting the tardy
morning, which is always late in getting down there, and
munches his dirty bit of bread as he comes along. His way
lying through many streets, and the houses not yet being
open, he sits down to breakfast on the doorstep of the
Society for the Propagation of the Gospel in Foreign Parts,
and gives it a brush when he has finished, as an acknow-
ledgment of the accommodation. He admires the size of the
edifice, and wonders what it's all about. He has no idea,
poor wretch, of the spiritual destitution of a coral reef in the
Pacific, or what it costs to look up the precious souls among
cocoa-nuts and bread-fruit.

But there is a third way of severing the gifts of Dickens from
what so powerfully shaped him: his childhood rejection – for
I think that Dickens is often at his greatest where no 'reaction'
can possibly be inferred. Nothing is here but the consummate
skill of a great artist, the eye of an observer of genius and the
skill and imagination to match it. Take, for example, Dickens'
description of the building of the London to Birmingham
Railroad – the M1 of the Victorian era:

Houses were knocked down; streets broken through and

stopped; deep pits and trenches dug in the ground; enormous heaps of earth and clay thrown up; buildings that were undermined and shaken, propped by great beams. Here, a chaos of carts, overthrown and jumbled together, lay topsy-turvy at the bottom of a steep unnatural hill; there, confused treasurers of iron soaked and rusted in something that had accidentally become a pond. Everywhere were bridges that led nowhere, and piles of scaffolding, and wildernesses of brick, and giant forms of cranes, and tripods straddling above nothing. Boiling water hissed and heaved within dilapidated walls; whence, also, the glare and roar of flames came issuing forth; and mounds of ashes blocked up rights of way, and wholly changed the law and custom of the neighbourhood.

It is on this railway that Mr Dombey, after the death of Paul, takes his journey to Leamington. And was there ever a better description in words of the passage of a train?

Through the hollow, on the height, by the heath, by the orchard, by the park, by the garden, over the canal, across the river, where the sheep are feeding, where the mill is going, where the barge is floating, where the dead are lying, where the factory is smoking . . . away, with a shriek, and a roar, and a rattle, and no trace to leave behind but dust and vapour . . . Louder and louder yet, it shrieks and cries as it comes tearing on resistless to the goal: and now its way, still like the way of Death, is strewn with ashes thickly. Everything around is blackened. There are dark pools of water, muddy lanes, and miserable habitation far below. There are jagged walls and falling houses close at hand, and through the battered roofs and broken windows, wretched rooms are seen, where want and fever hide themselves in many wretched shapes, while smoke and crowded gables, and distorted chimneys, and deformity of brick and mortar penning up deformity of mind and body, choke the murky distance. As Mr Dombey looks out of his carriage window, it is never in his thoughts that the monster who has brought him there has let the light of day in on these things: not made or caused them.

A last thought on Dickens. Had he been here today, what would he have talked on, preached on – with his pen? I suspect he would still be painting pictures: pictures of the homeless on our streets. I suspect his energies would have driven him in this generation all over the world wherever people are being ground down, and wherever people are laughing and living. I suspect he may be looking down from some corner of the ramparts of heaven today, gazing quizzically, and musing wistfully upon the diversity of human experience and human suffering and human joy. I hope he is directing his compassion towards those of us who profess and call ourselves Christian, whom I doubt would in our generation have convinced Dickens that we have a gospel of acceptance, that we are a community of compassion, that could heal his wounds and the wounds of his society anymore than the church in his age succeeded in convincing him.

One may dare at least to hope that in the life beyond this life, Charles Dickens has found a Heart that knows full well the bitterness of his heart and a Stranger who in being a Friend of infinite wisdom and unspeakable love, does not intermeddle with his joys, but increases them without end through the love that everlastingly he is.

12

'In the Beauty of the Lilies . . .'

Westminster Abbey; Whit Sunday, 26 May 1996

'In the beauty of the lilies . . .' Most of us – and especially any amongst us from America – will have no doubt who wrote those words, and when. Julia Ward Howe wrote them, for 'The Battle Hymn of the Republic', in 1861:

> Mine eyes have seen the glory of the coming of the Lord...
> *In the beauty of the lilies* Christ was born across the sea...

But John Updike, arguably the most distinguished writer of prose in the English-speaking world today, has recently chosen to use those six words, most imaginatively and sensitively, as the title for his latest work of fiction: *In the Beauty of the Lilies*. And I've little doubt that it will come to be regarded as one of the best novels of our time.

Before I let Updike speak for himself, this Whit Sunday afternoon, let me just ask you, who are gathered here today, to reflect on what wonderful creations we human beings are, who can ourselves create, by the gifts of the Spirit, such great works of literature, and who can be stirred and spoken to by such literature, such myths, as much as by, say, music. There, if you like, is the work and evidence of the Holy Spirit: the creating and redeeming Spirit.

For this seventeenth novel of his, Updike has chosen the greatest of all subjects: the dealings of God with humankind. He has ambitiously woven a tapestry of modern American history: of one imagined American family, the Wilmots. The first threads of that tapestry are woven to depict the mill-town of Paterson, New Jersey, on a hot afternoon in 1910, as the Reverend Clarence Wilmot, standing in the beautifully described rectory of the Fourth Presbyterian Church, experiences the last vestiges of his faith departing. He has allowed himself to be exposed to the modern forces of reason and science. Honourably, he resigns his very comfortable calling and position. He abandons the pulpit, to become an ineffectual salesman of popular encyclopaedias, in a Paterson now suffering a still-famous strike in its mills. Clarence Wilmot becomes a defeated and forsaken figure, haunting the motion picture houses of the day, for relief and for escape.

Yet I found myself concluding that the Holy Spirit was here, in the imagined, but by no means unrealistic figure of Clarence Wilmot: in his search for truth, his courageous struggle, and his utter integrity. And I felt I wanted the name of Clarence Wilmot to be heard here, in Westminster Abbey, this Whit Sunday afternoon.

The second subject of John Updike's tapestry, the second panel in his complex canvas and chronicle, concerns Clarence's son, Teddy. Influenced by his father's failure, blaming God for forsaking his father – as God had seemed to forsake Another, two thousand years before – Teddy rejects the 'chance of a life-time' in booming Manhattan, choosing instead a path which Updike describes in two words: 'minimal damage'. Teddy retreats, with the family, to become a postman, a mailman, in the small and obscure town of Basingstoke, Delaware, finally marrying the club-footed daughter of a market gardener. But, again, Updike so lovingly, caringly, observantly, describes the life of the postman and market gardener, that I had no doubt that I wanted to bring him also into this sacred shrine, this Whit Sunday. For that hidden and withdrawn figure seems to me, not least, to justify Updike's title:

In the beauty of the lilies Christ was born across the sea.
With a glory in his bosom that transfigures you and me.

Two brief quotations from Updike's novel:

Daddy let her come to the post office with its bright new mural of men with blue coats and pigtails that had to do with why Rodney Street was called that and watch him and Mr Horley sort the day's mail at the end of the day, tossing the letters into different sacks held up on some big pipe frames, for different parts of the country. Mr Horley could toss letters, twirling them by the edge, so far he could even get it in the sack for California, and never miss.

And a second sample of the simplicity of Updike's style and narrative:

The first summer that Teddy lived in Basingstoke the women could think of nothing better to do with the sole man of the house than have him dig up several summers' worth of weeds, break up the sod and shake the grass roots out of it, plant leaf lettuce and radishes and whatever other above-ground vegetables could come in after a late start, keep these rows hoed, and weed and harvest the asparagus bed. There was little art to asparagus, knowing when the tender purple-tinged nose, its leaflets overlapped like fish-scales, had poked enough inches out of the ground to be dug with the asparagus cutter, which was shaped like the tail of an arrow. Bunches of a dozen or so stalks were to be peddled fresh in the neighbourhood in the evenings. It was not unusual for the citizens of Basingstoke to sell each other produce; the dimes accumulated pleasantly in the pocket, and even some of the colored households – the better off who lived closer to town, in painted houses – were willing to buy. But the experience of going door to door reminded Teddy of his father's miserable year of encyclopedia-peddling.

There's an oft-quoted piece of Victorian verse which ex-claims:

Not God in gardens! . . .
Nay, but I have a sign
'Tis very sure God walks in mine.

Teddy, you feel, may have deserted church-going, in loyalty to
his father, yet the Spirit of God, all unseen, is close to him – as
he is to so many: and walks with him in his garden.

But the third section of Updike's great novel is on an altogether larger scale. Teddy's daughter, Essie, does a spell of
dubious modelling in New York, and eventually makes it to
Hollywood, where she becomes a star of the screen – Alma
DeMott – playing opposite Clark Gable and Bing Crosby. As
post-war history unfolds, she becomes, however, a Hollywood harlot, making many marriages, and is utterly obsessed
with her own image.

Updike is making his readers ask questions about God and
about the alternative gods and goddesses of America and,
indeed, of Western civilization: the gods of capitalism; the
gods of sex and of self, separated from any idea of the transcendent. I suggest again that Updike is asking questions
appropriately pursued here in this Abbey on Whit Sunday.

The fourth and final section of Updike's ambitious moral
and metaphysical history of America in the twentieth century
is centered upon Essie's only son, Clark. A neglected product
of Hollywood, he inherits his grandfather's instinct for
withdrawal, and retreats to a Colorado hippy commune: to a
fundamentalist religious community run by a charismatic who
owes much to David Koresh. Clark becomes the sect's PR
man, and the story ends with much millenarian promise and
verbiage, but, in tragic reality, with a siege by the state, ending
in a holocaust.

Updike, Malcolm Bradbury has pointed out, has often in his
novels explored the fate of faith and its secular alternatives in
the life of his nation 'founded on Protestant dreams but seeking new Utopias'.

On Whit Sunday, Updike's book confronts us with a series
of searching questions:

Where does the Holy Spirit lead us in 1996? – lead us as individuals, in our nations and societies, and in our churches – in our small towns and cities, like Hollywood, and our charismatic centres of promised renewal?

Does he lead us along the path of the Reverend Clarence Wilmot's painful yet clear-minded understanding of the modern challenge to faith?

Teddy's 'withdrawal' has something of the Spirit within it, yet no truly incarnational religion can be wholly about 'withdrawal'. Canon Max Warren, a one-time much-loved figure of this Abbey, in his book *The Truth of Vision,* fifty years ago drew attention to a passage in Arnold Toynbee's *A Study of History* in which he spoke of 'the principle of withdrawal *and return'*. During the period of withdrawal, Toynbee wrote, the personality is able 'to realize powers within himself which might have remained dormant if he had not been released for the time being from its social toils and trammels'. But, Toynbee continues: 'Withdrawal is an opportunity, and perhaps a necessary condition, for the anchorite's transfiguration'; 'anchorite', he reminds us, in the original Greek, means literally 'one who goes apart'; but 'a transfiguration in solitude', he says, 'can have no purpose, and, perhaps, even no meaning, except as a prelude to the return of the transfigured personality into the social milieu out of which he had originally come . . . This return is the essence of the whole movement . . . "Withdrawal with intent to return – until the Kingdom come".' That is, Max Warren maintains, the pattern of the ministry of Jesus himself, and is of immense significance, for the church and for every individual human being. It is, I suggest, by that example and by that principle of transfiguration that Teddy's withdrawal from life, but, even more, Clark's charismatic community, have to be judged.

In true withdrawal there is moral and metaphysical guidance for mankind. In true incarnation there is no less moral and metaphysical guidance for embodied individuals, whose sexual and emotional life is one of their most significant and God-given characteristics.

But on Whit Sunday, in this Abbey, we should surely also note how the disciples, before Pentecost, withdrew for fear – like Teddy and Clark – but how the gift of the Spirit enabled and empowered the disciples and the early church to return and confront the world around, and to serve and penetrate those surrounding cultures.

'In the beauty of the lilies Christ was born across the sea'
– and lived, and suffered, and died, and rose again –
'With a glory in his bosom that transfigures you and me.'

I have made little mention so far of the naive and simplistic pseudo-biblical fundamentalism that dominated the charismatic community to which Clark withdrew. But I think we should perhaps see the Reverend Clarence Wilmot as a truly charismatic figure. The Spirit is rarely a means of escape from the complexities of our human existence: from the tough and rigorous emotional, intellectual and spiritual problems of our humanity. The Spirit assists us – with groanings that cannot be uttered – towards mature humanity. He may, indeed, lead some to withdraw sometimes – temporarily – from, for instance, involvement in church-based ministry into an even greater calling and commitment and a deeper integrity, in a wider, even more needy world.

The last sentence of *In the Beauty of the Lilies* is of remarkable but significant brevity. It consists simply of two words: 'The children'. They are words of both vision and reality: 'The children' – black and white – of our cities – like Hollywood, Jersey City and London; 'the children' of our families, like the Wilmot family; 'the children' of our world: 'the children' of whom God is Father and Jesus Christ brother. 'The children' are the future. And the Spirit has created and redeemed them, and goes ahead of them: leading them, leading us, who are all of us still children of God, into the world that lies ahead. 'The children' are the future; and 'our God is marching on'.

13

The Dictionary of National Biography

Gray's Inn Chapel; 14 July 1996

'I will give thanks unto thee, for I am fearfully and wonderfully made.'

Psalm 139.13

There are two lines of poetry which, I imagine, most of us know: two lines of the great eighteenth-century poet, Alexander Pope, from his *Essay on Man*:

Know then thyself, presume not God to scan,
The proper study of mankind is man.

I not only believe in those words; I find that when someone asks me why I believe in God, I often respond by saying 'because I believe in and study man'.

It's that conviction, and that approach to belief, that has surfaced and asserted itself recently as I have mulled over the latest volume of the Dictionary of National Biography, which covers the years 1986–1990. It thudded on to my door-mat a couple of weeks ago because I had been responsible for one of the entries, and mercifully you get a free copy as reward for your labour. Some of the entries remind me of people I've known, but others I've met only through the pages of the DNB. All I propose to do this morning is to select one or two of those entries and let them speak for themselves, and let them comment on my text: 'I will give thanks unto thee, for I am fearfully and wonderfully made.'

Take, for instance the Baroness Lane-Fox, whom I never

myself met. Here's part of the entry, written by Sir Edward
Ford, who has been Secretary of the Order of Merit since
1975. (He was one of the sons of Lionel Ford, one-time
Headmaster of Repton, then of Harrow, and then Dean of
York.)

LANE-FOX, Felicity, champion of the disabled, was born 22
June 1918 in Newton Kyme, near Tadcaster, Yorkshire, the
youngest child in the family of one son and three daughters
of Captain Edward Lane-Fox, JP, and his wife, Enid Maud
Bethell . . . At the age of two, Felicity developed periostitis,
which left her with a permanently weak right arm. In 1930,
at the age of twelve, on a summer holiday on the Yorkshire
coast at Filey, she contracted poliomyelitis in a vicious
form, which left her totally paralysed. Two years passed
before she was able to sit up or hold a cup or pencil.

During this period she was living at home in the family
house near Wetherby. Deprived of any formal education,
she acquired knowledge by her own efforts supported by
her mother's wide-ranging enthusiasms. Her mother, who
lived until 1986, devoted the next fifty-five years of her life
to the daily care of her crippled daughter. After her mother
became incapable of looking after her, she was cared for by
her sister.

When war came in 1939. Felicity Lane-Fox took on a job
with the billeting officer in Wetherby. After the end of
hostilities in 1945 she went into local politics as a councillor for the Wetherby division of the West Riding county
council and became chairman of the local Conservative
Association. Her interest in politics took her from there in
1960 to an appointment as assistant at the Conservative
Research Department and in 1963 she became a member of
the executive of the National Union of Conservative and
Unionist Associations. Through these links with the party,
she became known to Margaret (later Baroness) Thatcher,
who, on becoming prime minister, offered her in 1981 a life
peerage, which she was only persuaded to accept after her

mother convinced her that the House of Lords would give her a forum for speaking on behalf of the disabled. This she assiduously did during the next seven years, making her maiden speech, a fortnight after taking her seat, on the integration of disabled children into ordinary schools. She was absent from the House on only three working days during her first year as a member.

Her work for the disabled had already won her an OBE in 1976, for in spite of her own disability, and with the indefatigable help of her mother, who combined the roles of nurse, chauffeuse, and counsellor, she travelled widely, spoke frequently, and carried on a large correspondence on behalf of a number of societies and projects connected with disabled people. Among these were the Nuffield Orthopaedic Centre at Oxford, where she was a member of the house committee, and the national fund-raising committee of the Disablement Income Group, of which she was chairman. In 1978 she became patron of the Handicapped Adventure Playground Association. To all these activities she paid full attention, regularly attending their meetings, to which she was driven in a specially adapted minicar into which she could be winched through the back window by her mother, who in spite of increasing age managed to propel her in the vehicle or on the ground with unflagging energy. For having learned to walk with the aid of a caliper and some human support, Felicity Lane-Fox in 1966 slipped on an icy patch of roadway, broke her pelvis, and was never able to walk again.

After becoming a baroness she accepted several further appointments to societies for the disabled, in particular becoming a member of the Prince of Wales' advisory group on disability and the committee of inquiry into arts and disabled people. But the project which was closest to her heart was the Phipps Respiratory Unit Patients' Association (PRUPA). This unit, originally established in Clapham by Dr Geoffrey Spencer to provide relief and therapy for patients suffering from breathing maladies, was, thanks to her fund-raising efforts, later moved to become part of St Thomas' Hospital in Lambeth Palace Road, where it was renamed the Lane-Fox Respiratory Unit, and is a fitting memorial to her.

Felicity Lane-Fox leavened her arduous work for the disabled by a variety of other interests. She enjoyed watching cricket, tennis, racing, drama, and documentaries on television or listening to them on the radio, as well as a game of bridge and perhaps, most of all, social intercourse and conversation with her many friends. Her life was an example of how to overcome crippling physical infirmity and use the experience of it to alleviate the plight of fellow sufferers.

The fact that she was chair-bound, and also possessed a mane of thick brown hair, made it appear that her head was unusually large. With a high forehead, mischievous grey eyes, a classical nose, and a magnolia complexion, which never showed signs of ageing, her face gave an impression of being poised for laughter, into which it readily dissolved. She died unmarried in St Thomas' Hospital 17 April 1988.

After reading that marvellous entry by Sir Edward Ford do I have to do more than repeat my text: 'I will give thanks unto thee, for I am fearfully and wonderfully made'? Anyone reading that potted biography must surely ask, 'Where did all those wonderful gifts come from?'

But now I want to turn to an entry which relates to someone very familiar to many of you. So too is the author of the entry. There are, of course, a number of members of Gray's Inn to be found in this volume of the DNB: people like our erstwhile Treasurer 'Jack' Hampson, whose entry is penned by Master Jolowicz (I was privileged to know 'Jack' Hampson and Tony Jolowicz at Cambridge as well as here). But I have chosen as my second subject someone whom it is difficult to believe left us seven years ago: Baron Elwyn-Jones. The writer of the entry is Emlyn Hooson.

Again let me read part of that entry:

JONES, Elwyn, lawyer and politician, was born 24 October 1909 in Llanelli, the youngest in the family of three sons and a daughter of Frederick Jones, tin-plate rollerman, and his wife Elizabeth Griffiths, daughter of a small farmer from Carmarthenshire. His father was a greatly respected member of the local community, an elder of the Tabernacle Congregational chapel, and a lifelong socialist, and his mother had an immensely strong and influential personality. The three other children all achieved success, in the worlds of science, business, and education respectively. Elwyn-Jones was educated at Llanelli Grammar School, the University College of Wales at Aberystwyth, and Gonville and Caius College, Cambridge, where he became president of the Cambridge Union. In the Cambridge history tripos he obtained a first-class in part i and a second class in part ii. He went on to Gray's Inn and was called to the bar in 1935.

With his intense concern for human freedom and justice, he became politically involved with the Fabians and it was through this connection that he responded to a request to go out and give legal help to the beleaguered Austrian Social Democrats during the time of the chancellorship of Engelbert Dollfuss (1932–34). It was then that he became greatly involved with the European problem and attended political trials in Germany, Greece, Hungary, and Romania, organizing help for those accused. He wrote to various newspapers about the problems and went on to write three books for the Left Book Club on the Fascist threat.

In the late 1930s Elwyn-Jones rejected his earlier pacifism as the answer to the Nazi menace and became a Territorial Army volunteer. During World War II he served as major in the Royal Artillery in North Africa and Italy but ended the war as deputy judge advocate, attending many courts martial and inquiries into alleged Nazi brutalities. Following his election to Parliament in 1945, as Labour MP for Plaistow (West Ham), he soon became parliamentary private secretary to the attorney-general, Sir Hartley Shawcross, and joined the team of counsel for the prosecution at the Nuremberg war crimes trials.

In 1949 he was appointed recorder of Merthyr Tydfil; he took silk in 1953. He became recorder of Swansea in 1953, of Cardiff in 1960, the year he became a bencher of Gray's Inn, and of Kingston upon Thames in 1968. In the meantime he was reasonably active politically (as MP for West Ham South from 1950 to 1974) but still devoted a good deal of time to his practice on the Wales and Chester circuit. However, following the Labour victory in the 1964 general election, Elwyn-Jones became attorney-general, holding that position until 1970, throughout the Labour government.

During his period as attorney-general, in co-operation with the Lord Chancellor, Gerald Gardiner, the most important achievement was the establishment in 1965 of the Law Commission, under the chairmanship of Sir Leslie Scarman. As attorney-general, Elwyn-Jones was also counsel for the tribunal in the Aberfan inquiry, when over a hundred children had been killed in a Welsh village school by the movement of a coal slurry tip. He prosecuted in the Moors murder case and in cases arising from the Official Secrets Act.

Following the fall of the Labour government in 1970 he returned to his legal practice, by then mainly in London. When Labour returned in 1974, Elwyn-Jones became lord chancellor, with a life peerage, and severed his longstanding tie with his beloved East End constituency. As lord chancellor he encouraged the growth of law centres, whose number had quadrupled by the time he left office.

Although a lord chancellor (until 1979, when he became lord of appeal) and attorney-general of distinction, he was not a profound lawyer. Law as such was not his prime interest; politics were. He was very much a political lawyer of swift intelligence, good judgment, and rare sensibility; more concerned that the legal system should provide the means of achieving true justice than with handing down great judgments himself.

Elwyn-Jones was a member of the Bar Council and chairman of the Society of Labour Lawyers. He was president of University College, Cardiff, from 1971 to 1988. He was an honorary fellow of his Cambridge college and received six honorary degrees. A privy councillor from 1964, he was knighted in the same year and appointed CH in 1976.

Elwyn-Jones was tall and dark-haired, with aquiline features and a ready smile. He was a man of natural charm and dignity, with a warm personality, convivial disposition, and fine sense of humour. He was a superb raconteur and had a very fine light baritone singing voice, with which he entertained his friends and which he sometimes used on formal occasions. There was a disarming simplicity about his approach, and his shrewdness and capacity to grasp the essential points of a controversy, hidden behind an approach of urbanity and charming whimsicality, were often used to take the heat out of Commons debates, which might otherwise have become acrimonious. However, below the surface were to be found the true convictions from which he never wavered. When put to the test, his concern for social justice would manifest itself in passionate outbursts.

In 1937 he married Pearl ('Polly'), daughter of Morris Binder, a Jewish tailor in Salford. They had one son and two daughters. Pearl Binder was a lively and versatile writer, artist, radio and television personality, and expert on costume. The marriage was very happy. Elwyn-Jones died in Brighton 4 December 1989 and his wife died seven weeks later.

I well remember conducting Elwyn's funeral and his burial in the City of London cemetery, within Elwyn's former constituency, where it happens that my father is also buried.

My question is: Did Elwyn-Jones just 'happen', so to speak? Was that unique biography of his the product simply of a complex mechanistic world? Or is my text a more appropriate way of approaching such a creation: 'I will give thanks unto thee, for I am fearfully and wonderfully made'?

The third and last entry which I want to quote is, in fact, the one I wrote myself. Janet Lacey I knew from my school days in Dagenham, in the 1930s, to her death in 1988; and I was privileged to preach at her memorial service in St Martin-in-the-Fields.

LACEY, Janet, director of Christian Aid, was born in Sunderland 25 October 1903, the younger child and younger daughter of Joseph Lacey, property agent, who had been born within the sound of Bow Bells, and his wife, Elizabeth Smurthwaite, from the north of England. Her father died when Janet was ten and her sister, Sadie, died of cancer in mid-life. She went to various schools in Sunderland before going to drama school in Durham. Her family were fairly narrow Methodists, mostly teetotal, though her father 'drank whisky like water'. It may have been her father's death which caused Janet's mother to send her to live with an aunt in Durham.

Although she toured in the theatre world for three years, Janet Lacey found it hard to make a living. At the age of twenty-two she applied to the Young Women's Christian Association for work, and in 1926 was sent to the YWCA at Kendal to train as a youth leader. She stayed there for six years. Her skills in drama were fully used, and she received her first introduction to theology. During the General Strike of 1926 she saw much poverty in Durham pit villages and became a Labour supporter. In 1932 she moved to Dagenham, to a job which used many of her gifts, in a mixed YMCA-YWCA community centre at the heart of a vast new housing estate which provided activities 'from the cradle to the grave'.

In 1945 she became YMCA education secretary to the British Army of the Rhine, which was slowly being demobilized. It was typical of her that she used the post to bring young British soldiers together with young Germans and with refugees. She learned much about running programmes of social aid and made her first contacts with ecumenical church leaders like Bishop Hans Lilje and Bishop George Bell. She said she would go about whispering to herself: 'I must not get used to this devastation.' Her capacity for compassion shaped her career.

She was appointed youth secretary of the British Council of Churches in 1947, a job which introduced her to the World Council of Churches. She was a significant presence at its four assemblies: at Amsterdam, Evanston, New Delhi, and Uppsala. For the second assembly she wrote and produced a dramatic presentation, *By the Waters of Babylon*. She got to know intimately many of the leaders of the world church, such as Visser t'Hooft. In Britain the peak of her work was the Bangor youth conference in 1951.

By 1952 Janet Lacey needed a task which would use her full talents. In December that year she was appointed secretary (the term director was only used later) of Inter-Church Aid (from 1960 Christian Aid), a post she held until 1968. She worked from both Geneva and London, helping to establish many other important bodies such as Voluntary Service Overseas and World Refugee Year, but her greatest contribution was to conceive Christian Aid Week. This was wholly her idea and she executed it with characteristic flair. The first week raised only £25,000 but by the time she retired it was raising £2 million a year. 'Need not creed' was Janet Lacey's slogan as she stumped not only Britain but the world.

She was tough and stocky; without being tall she confronted others as being a tower of strength. She was a formidable, autocratic leader, often infuriating, but her compassion in action caused even her critics to admire her. She was blunt to a fault. She was a skilled manager, but not as humane in her management as the really good manager needs to be, so that after she retired from Christian Aid, her years as director of the Family Welfare Association were not a total success. She more successfully reorganized the Churches' Council for Health and Healing. Although she could run huge organizations, she could not boil an egg: nevertheless she loved entertaining her friends – at restaurants. She adored the theatre, music, and sculpture.

After her great contribution to World Refugee Year, she was appointed CBE in 1960. In 1967 she became the first woman to preach in St Paul's Cathedral. In 1970 her autobiographical volume *A Cup of Water* was published. Later in life she was prepared for confirmation by Father St John Groser, the socialist East End priest. She was awarded an honorary DD from Lambeth in 1975. Her retirement in her Westminster flat was happy – she would welcome her many friends from all corners of the globe – until she became a victim of Alzheimer's disease. She died in a Kensington nursing home, 11 July 1988, after having spent several years living there. She never married.

I have personal reasons for giving thanks that Janet Lacey was 'fearfully and wonderfully made'; but so, too, have many people around the world. I so well remember, when visiting Uganda in 1972, in the first years of Amin's evil regime, going to the Kitwe Community Centre, in the heart of the worst slums of Kampala. I'd rarely been so impressed with a centre. There was a primary school, a clinic, adult education, youth work, trades teaching, and so on. It was financed jointly by the Uganda Christian Council, Oxfam, and Christian Aid. As I walked through the crowded and busy buildings, I suddenly caught sight of the foundation stone, with its engraved letters: 'This foundation stone was laid by Janet Lacey, Director of Christian Aid', and the day, the month and the year, 1963; and my heart missed a beat at seeing Janet's name, and then gave a kind of lift of affection and proud thanksgiving. 'I will give thanks unto thee, for *she* was fearfully and wonderfully made.'

As our second lesson this morning from the Epistle to the Hebrews said, 'What shall I more say? For the time would fail me to tell of Gedeon, and of Barak, and of Samson, and of Jepthae; of David also, and Samuel, and of the prophets . . .'

What should I more say today? For the time would fail me to tell, as I've said, of other members of Gray's Inn in that volume of the DNB; and of people like Michael Ramsey, formerly Archbishop of Canterbury. There's an entry by Yehudi Menuhin for Jacqueline du Pré, to whom one day I had to take my young Indian 'cellist friend, Anup Biswas, and his accompanist. I can't forget Jacqueline du Pré, in her wheelchair, saying to Anup, after his accompanist had played the introduction to a Beethoven sonata: 'What were you doing while Christopher was playing that introduction?' And Anup replying, as though there was no other possible answer to the question, 'I was waiting to come in'; and Jacqueline replying gently, 'You should have been suffering with him and waiting to comfort him.'

Of course, these entries in the DNB record a great deal of suffering of one sort and another. Jacqueline du Pré, it says, at times 'gave way to depression'. There is quite a lot of evil in the entries, not far below the surface. Our capacity for evil as well as for good is part of our being 'fearfully and wonderfully made'; so, too, is our capacity to struggle with evil, and to be delivered from it, and to triumph over it.

I suspect someone may want to say: 'The DNB is a very elitist volume, isn't it?' And it undoubtedly is. But it isn't merely about the high born. It's about people of low birth – if we may use such a term – who, like Janet Lacey, achieved high awards, like the CBE.

I myself think it would be only a cynic who dismissed the DNB, or who said 'Yes: those in the DNB are fearfully and wonderfully made but they are the exceptions.' The whole point of my sermon this morning is, in fact, to draw from you your own personal conclusion and reflection that you are 'fearfully and wonderfully made', and that so, too, are all those on, let us say, the top of a Clapham omnibus. And, this particular week, let us add that Nelson Mandela is fearfully and wonderfully made, but so too, did they but know it, are those who imprisoned him; and so too are those too who, tragically, yesterday, planted again a bomb on the streets of Enniskillen. So it is appropriate to end '*In the name of the Father* . . .'

14

The Alabaster Box

St Stephen's, Rochester Row; 4 August 1996

It's very good to return here to St Stephen's where I was a curate in the 1950s. I celebrated holy communion for the first time at Michaelmas 1952. The altar was decked with Michaelmas daisies provided by Cecily Gregson, who bought at Oberammergau that crucifix above the pulpit. My vicar, George Reindorp, put a red line through every page of my first sermon. He quickly despatched me to the Abbey School of Speakers to have my voice seen to. I have to admit my pride was hurt, but I endeavoured not to show it.

But what I hadn't bargained for was just how much I'd get out of the exercise, and I don't mean in terms of the improvement of my voice and delivery. You see, the man who took charge of me based almost all his tuition, for several weeks, on the Collect for Purity, at the beginning of the 1662 communion service.

He said to me: 'Just read the first prayer for me.' I hadn't got further than 'Almighty God . . .' when he stopped me and asked 'What were you thinking of when you said those two words "Almighty God . . ."?' I was rather flummoxed by the question.'Would you mind saying them again,' he said, 'and this time will you think of all the words "Almighty God" mean to you?' I did, and went on to the following words '. . . to whom all hearts be open, all desires known, and from whom no secrets are hid,' thinking of all that those words meant. My instructor then said: 'You have got to say the words in such a way that those who hear you will catch something of what the words mean to you.'

He asked me to say that one prayer dozens of times before he allowed me to move on to anything else; and I realized that he was much more than a speech trainer. I often think of him when I come to the words of today's Gospel: 'Not everyone that saith unto me "Lord, Lord . . ."' We have to hear the words so profoundly that they deeply affect our whole being and our every thought and action. It's no good just rushing the words 'Almighty God' or 'Lord'.

Those eight verses in St Matthew's Gospel – chapter 26 vv. 6–13 – describe one of the most beautiful incidents in our Lord's life. And its beauty and pathos are heightened because we know that tragedy, the tragedy of Holy Week, waits in the wings.

Jesus is at Bethany in the house of Simon, 'the leper'. Perhaps the name is witness to some marvel of the healing power of Christ; perhaps Jesus had helped Simon to live with, come to terms with, his leprosy, with its stigma. Perhaps Simon was *once* a leper. He'd known what it *was* to suffer and be a social reject, like someone with AIDS today.

I can never now hear the word 'leper' without thinking of a little community, all of whom had suffered from leprosy, all of whom had been beggars on the streets of Delhi, till the city authorities had decided to sweep the streets clean of beggars and they had been put in a compound outside the city, across the Jamuna river. It was nearly twenty-five years ago, in 1972, that Amos Rajamoni, a young priest of the Brotherhood of the Ascension, took me with him to celebrate Holy Communion for some of them. And as we approached the gates, some crawled towards us, with stumps for arms and legs, or no arms and legs, and some were blind. But I can't forget the joy with which they greeted Amos – and me, as his friend – because Amos had so clearly accepted them. I visited them again, six years later. Amos, with his skills, not only as a priest but in community development, had helped them to recover their self-respect. I've never seen such a transformed – healed – community: though clearly they were still what they had been – lepers.

Well, you'll understand that the phrase 'in the house of Simon, the leper' carries now for me what they call 'particular resonances'. But while Jesus was having a meal with his friends there, a woman came to him with an alabaster jar of the 'most expensive ointment', and poured it on his head.

You can read the story in Mark as well as Matthew and Luke. You can read it in John, but there the woman is named Mary, and her sister Martha is serving, and Lazarus is living there – whom Jesus raised from the dead – and Judas is named as the one who objected to what happened.

In St Luke you can read the story in a rather different context. It's a Pharisee's house, and the woman has been living an immoral life.

In Matthew and in Mark, the anointing is to prepare Jesus 'for burial'. It foreshadows and foretells Christ's death. And Jesus says: 'Wherever in all the world this Good News is proclaimed, what she has done will be told also in remembrance of her.'

Well, if all the Gospels had some record of it – with variations – that saying certainly came true. You can say it has come true this morning as we remember the story. And even today, it is, I think, one of the most moving stories in all the Gospels. A scene is set before us with the consummate skill of a great artist: a Rembrandt.

As an onlooker on the scene – even with two thousand years between – I find it's difficult not to be moved. Here is someone responding to Jesus with a thankful overflowing heart. The scene is so vividly described, you can almost smell it. But you can see that it stinks in the nostrils of some of the observers. Yet their objection calls forth a soft answer from Jesus: 'Why trouble ye the woman . . . ?'

It's an extraordinary scene. It takes a Johann Sebastian Bach to cope with it; and those of you who are familiar with his *St Matthew Passion* will know how marvellously Bach has in fact set it to music. No one would invent this incident. It's a scene of extravagance: of extravagant love. To the disciples, or certainly to one of them, it's wasteful.

We don't know whether this woman intended or planned to do what she did: whether it was a premeditated act – a present, carefully bought and given – or whether it was sudden and spontaneous. But, at some moment, her hands moved with her heart. We would say these days she was literally 'in touch with her feelings'. Her hands moved to the lid, and prized it open, and spilt the contents, and the whole house was filled with the scent. No one could pretend it hadn't happened.

It's an action of self-forgetful boldness. It doesn't seem calculated: rather the opposite. It's an expensive, expansive action. (And if she was an immoral woman – and in a leper's house – well, it's all the more marvellous – or upsetting – according to where you stand.)

As I read it, it fills me with admiration and envy, and quite a bit of guilt that such devotion as *I* have has a kind of corrupting care about it. I'm frankly incapable – I feel – of devotion anything like that – to Jesus. There's something in this incident of the flame of God's love: not just a flicker.

But as an onlooker – as I get involved in the scene – I realize that God has, so-to-speak, put into my hand an alabaster box; but, where devotion is concerned, I'm a creature of fear, respectability, self-consciousness, self-centredness and boredom. A voice within says: 'Prize open the alabaster box!' But it's too much. And I'm left moved, but, even more, envious of that woman.

It's, of course, one of the most 'full-bodied', so to speak – indeed one of the most sexual – incidents in the Gospels.

The former Bishop of Woolwich, the late John Robinson, in his book *The Human Face of God*, remarks that most ministers today would not be able to survive three circumstantial – and independent – reports that he had had his feet (or his head) kissed, scented and wiped with the hair of a woman, whether or not of doubtful repute. The lack of defensiveness with which such compromising stories are told of Jesus – John Robinson adds – says a great deal.

Who is this person, to whom this deed is done? Who is this

person – in relation to our devotion – and to the alabaster box which the Lord has put into my hands and yours?

Not so long ago, I was asked to preach a very difficult sermon. The parish priest said, 'Will you come and preach on "Why do I pray and how?"' It ought to have been simple; but it was without doubt one of the most difficult and most searching subjects I'd been asked to preach on for several years – to preach on it honestly. It made me reflect on my own devotional 'autobiography': my own 'alabaster box'.

I can't remember my own very first prayers. But I can recall my first memory of my prayers. I can remember Mrs Hasler, the kindly superintendent of the Methodist Sunday School where I was taken as a toddler; and I can remember her saying: 'Now close your peepers' – after she had said 'Hands together and eyes closed'. And, after a silence, I can remember her saying: 'There's one little boy who still hasn't closed his peepers.' And I expect you can guess who that little boy was.

I had religious parents, and I learnt very early on about certain sorts of prayer, and that it was a matter of closing your eyes.

It was at least twenty years later that I began to learn very different things about prayer. And now – nearly another fifty years later – grateful as I am for my Methodist upbringing, I would describe my prayer in a very different way from the way prayer was first described to me.

I was in fact a classic late-developer, and was taken away from school when I was fourteen, not least because I was such a dud and a dunce; and I came round to things like Shakespeare at night-school, when I was trying to make up for lost time. And I can remember then coming across a phrase in Shakespeare's *King Lear* which suddenly seemed to open up new worlds for me, not least new worlds of prayer.

King Lear, when he has gone through much suffering, invites his daughter Cordelia – with him – to

> take upon's the mystery of things,
> As if we were God's spies.

Since, roughly, the time I came across that phrase of
Shakespeare's, prayer has become to me primarily and over-
whelmingly doing just that: taking upon me the mystery of
things as if I were one of God's spies. And I find it important
to do that in lots of different ways, at different times, and in
different places.

Music, for instance, has always meant a lot to me: listening
to it, and playing the piano or the organ, is for me often
'taking upon me the mystery of things'. Of course, it means
working at getting the notes right and getting my fingers to do
what I tell them. But I don't know what I'd do without music
– without music interpreting the 'mystery of things': not solv-
ing it, but plumbing it a bit more from time to time: sometimes
simply celebrating it. Music has played a large part in my
devotional life. Perhaps a piano, or organ, is my alabaster box.

The work of a priest in, for instance, taking baptisms,
weddings and funerals is very obviously taking upon us the
mystery of things: being what St Paul calls a 'steward of the
mysteries of God'. But I want to suggest that every human
being, ordained or lay, whatever our job, is involved, through
birth, marriage, suffering, death and friendship, in 'taking
upon us the mystery of things as if we were God's spies'.

In my little garden in Kennington, just over Lambeth
Bridge, I have a climber called a Bignonia which, at the
moment, has scarlet trumpets on it. It's blossoming between
my house and the block of flats in Kennington Lane at the
back of me. Just to look at that Bignonia in bloom – and the
poet Housman says that 'to look at things in bloom fifty
Springs are little room' – to look at that Bignonia in bloom, or
a dahlia or a rose, is to take upon me the mystery of things.

But life isn't all roses and Bignonias in bloom. The mystery
of things includes the mystery of evil as well as the mystery
of good, and the mystery of evil is quite as profound as the
mystery of God.

Some of you will know that a few years ago I wrote
the biography of Bishop John Robinson, whom I've already
mentioned. I was interested to discover that in only his second

sermon – as a deacon – he had said that you have to discover God in cancer. He said that 'it's no good thinking of a world outside God's creating and redeeming power'. Later, John Robinson had to live out those words as he died.

Mentioning John Robinson reminds me how much of my devotional life is related to the mystery of friendship and of human relating. I expect you all know what it's like once in a while to know yourself very close to someone – that's the mystery of things. But sometimes, when you're feeling close to someone, you're aware that no matter how close you get, there's a kind of sea of separateness surrounding each one of us, even an ocean. That's also the mystery of things: something God-given. Maybe the Ocean is God.

Sometimes our sexuality makes us very much like animals, which in many ways we are. Sometimes we can reverence one another through our sexuality, in ways which make us know that sex is one of God's chief ways of enabling us to 'take upon us the mystery of things'. This incident of the woman with the alabaster box ought to say something to us of a devotion and worship which includes and takes up our sexuality. Our sexuality is part of our alabaster box.

My day-to-day job, some of you will know, is to run a charity called Christian Action. People often ask me: 'What does Christian Action do?' 'Oh,' I say, 'it's to do with justice and peace.' 'Really?' they say.' Yes,' I say. 'It's to do with justice, not least in the inner cities – through housing, education, employment, race, and so on.' And I often add: 'Archbishop William Temple said that justice is the first requirement of love.' I try not to say much more, because I want people to see that when you deal with love and justice you take upon yourself the mystery of things; but you have to do it in very down-to-earth ways: most often, of course, in bringing up a family and housing them. Devotion to justice and love is all in 'the alabaster box'.

But the heart of the mystery for a Christian – a door that opens on to the mystery – is the eventually triumphant suffering of Jesus. It's the best spy hole on the mystery I know; and every time we come to holy communion we have another opportunity to 'take upon us the mystery of things as if we were God's spies'. As we think upon the pain of Christ, we get closer to the pain of the world. And wherever we encounter the pain of the world we find that the pain of Christ interprets it: profoundly comments upon this mystery of things.

It is in response to the divine mystery that we are invited to 'prize open the alabaster box' of our heart: our feelings, our body and mind, our intellect and our soul.

God in Christ enables us who are human to prize open the mysterious 'alabaster box' that is uniquely ours. And I suggest today that you think out what is the mysterious alabaster box that is uniquely yours.

15

In Memoriam: Archie Gordon

The Chapel, Haddo House; 8 September 1996

'We bring our years to an end, as it were a tale that is told.'
Psalm 90.9

I doubt whether there's a greater human gift than the gift of story-telling. I only have to mention the name of, say, John Buchan . . . But then there are our own stories, those of our families, our friends, and of places familiar and unfamiliar.

Recently, I was given a book I specially wanted to read, as I'd known and loved the author, and had been privileged to say the prayers at his memorial service in St Margaret's, Westminster.

Mark Bonham Carter, besides being a publisher and a Member of Parliament, was the first chairman of the Race Relations Board, and in that office was a most courageous pioneer for justice. I knew he had edited *The Autobiography of Margot Asquith,* but I only recently learnt he'd also edited the diaries and letters of her step-daughter, his mother, Violet Bonham Carter, the first volume of which – those from 1904 to 1914 – was published earlier this year. He had called it *Lantern Slides* because, in her diary for 27 December 1910, she had written: 'How strange it would be and how frightening if one could see isolated scenes of one's life in advance, like lantern-slides, without knowing where they were or when, what led up to them or what followed.'

As the eldest daughter of the Liberal Leader and Prime Minister, Asquith, and, as I say, the step-daughter of the remarkable Margot Asquith, Violet Bonham Carter was, of course, in a privileged position. *Lantern Slides* opens with the very first entry in her diary, begun in Paris, when she was only seventeen. She writes of being presented at Court, of grand dances, of political intrigue. But I don't think it was simply that I knew I would shortly be coming to preach here which made for me the most moving pages those which described the death from a motoring accident of one of her closest friends, Archie Gordon, son of the seventh Earl of Aberdeen. It was when I had read those pages that my text came to mind: 'We bring our years to an end, as it were a tale that is told.'

It was on the last Sunday in November 1909 that Archie Gordon was fatally injured in that accident, just outside Winchester. He was driving his brand-new Daimler towards Chippenham when he collided with a Renault, at a badly sighted crossroad. Archie's car overturned, trapping him underneath. He sustained severe injuries to his abdomen, and was taken by horse-drawn carriage to the Royal County Hospital in Winchester. Archie was, in fact, the only person seriously hurt in the accident. Violet Bonham Carter was staying in Oxfordshire at the time of the accident, and travelled to Winchester the following Saturday. She was not allowed to see Archie until the early hours of the following Wednesday, 15 December, when it was clear he was losing his battle for life.

I want first to read you a page or two from Violet Bonham Carter's diary covering those days, written later that December, 1909, when she was twenty-two. She begins:

I am going to try and write down as simply and as accurately as I can everything that I remember of the greatest day of my life. At 10 (pm) I drove up to the Hospital . . . and ran upstairs to Lady Aberdeen. The wind was howling . . . in about 10 minutes the Drs came out of A's room. They were silent at first; I thought the usual measured and judicial evolution of the bulletin was in process and tried not to interrupt. Presently I tugged Godwin (the surgeon's) coat and said: 'Do let it be "progress" – I'm so tired of the day before yesterday's improvement being maintained.' He looked at us compassionately and then away – then with difficulty he told us that heart-failure had set in and that the outlook was very grave. I asked if there was any hope and saw at once in his eyes that there was none. I think Lady Aberdeen still had a flicker . . . Godwin promised I should see A before he became unconscious – and said he might live till the morning. From 11 to 4 I watched our precious sands running out – then they came to tell me I might go in to him.

He had asked for me during the day and Godwin told him I was passing thro' Winchester and would come now. He didn't seem to think it strange – he said: 'You'll get her here for me all right Dr won't you? – I don't look bad do I? Give me a little brandy before she comes in to buck me up – put a good high cushion on the chair so that I can see her properly.' When they said: 'you may go in now', I felt the greatest joy I have ever known. I could not see beyond it . . . Godwin took me in.

The first thing I was conscious of was dim light and an all-pervasive smell of Eau-de-Cologne – then I saw Archie – propped up in bed by pillows on every side – his face changed and transfigured beyond recognition – his breathing coming and going in short, sharp gasps – his arms held out to me . . . he lay back breathlessly and I kissed him. Then I sat down beside him and held his hands while he asked me 10,000 questions – how I had come – why they had let me – wasn't it too late for me etc. etc. When I had satisfied him that it was quite a normal proceeding I said I had something to tell him – only he mustn't allow it to excite or tire him. Then I told him in the words Heaven sent me for such a moment that I loved him – that everything I had to give was his . . .

I called Godwin and said 'Dr, Archie wishes me to tell you we're going to be married' – A (said): 'Yes tho' perhaps at first sight I don't look it Dr I am at this moment in the most enviable position of any man alive. And she's *cured* me Dr. I could walk now – I can't *feel* the beastly pelvis or

the rib – no pain – no breathlessness – I'm treading on air
. . .'

Godwin came in and gave him heroin, a derivative of
morphia . . . he said: 'Dr, fancy being engaged' – and then
went off wonderfully quickly into a sort of drugged sleep
with his eyes half-open but his mind apparently at rest . . .

Archie died of heart failure at twenty minutes to seven on
the morning of Thursday 16 December 1909. A memorial
service for him was held in the Temple Church in London the
following Monday. He lay here in the Chapel before he was
buried in the cemetery on Thursday 23rd. A large congregation of friends and family weathered a heavy snowfall to be
present, and were joined by a deputation of the tenants and
estate employees. The pall-bearers included three members of
the government – H. H. Asquith, the Prime Minister, Lord
Aberdeen and Lord Pentland, as well as two ex-ministers.
Archie's brothers, George and Dudley, and his cousin, Jasper
Ridley, completed the group. Despite the recent bad weather,
the day itself was fine, and the carriage bearing Archie made
its way from this Chapel to the cemetery in bright sunlight.
Violet followed between Lord and Lady Aberdeen. Her
parting gesture was to cast a wreath of violets into the grave,
bearing the inscription 'To my beloved'.

'We bring our years to an end, as it were a tale that is told'.
Archibald Ian Gordon, youngest son of the Earl of Aberdeen,
– undoubtedly his mother's favourite son – was twenty-five
when he died. His room in the Royal Hampshire County
Hospital was later named 'The Gordon Room' in his memory.

What has surprised and delighted me is that, also in
memory of Archie, in the autumn of 1910, Violet formed a
kind of boys' club, called the Archie Gordon Club, which met
in the Maurice Institute in Hoxton, in the East End of London.
Lots of different memorials had been proposed – stained glass,
and stone, and so on – but Violet set her heart on this kind of
club, devoted to giving a start in life to a number of lads whose
home conditions were otherwise too hopeless to give them a

fair chance. The boys were recruited individually through school Care Committees. The Maurice Institute, where they met, was a settlement which had been set up by the Christian Social Union. Running the club – from, let it be noted, 10 Downing Street – helped Violet, probably more than anything else, to overcome the loss of Archie.

From late December 1909 until June 1913, Violet's diary entries took the form of letters addressed to Archie, generally beginning 'Beloved', or 'My Darling', and ending 'Your Own', or simply 'Yours'. I'd like to read you just one or two paragraphs from those entries.

First, the entry for 10 November 1910.

My Darling – Just back from the second Club night – it was just as gloriously successful as the first – and made better by a close intimacy with the members – 'poor little fellows' – they really do come under this comprehensive heading. They contrive to be marvellously happy on wonderfully little. Each one has a skeleton in his family cupboard which has carefully to be avoided – I blunder heavily on them now and then. 'Jenkins – you can take these flowers home for your Mother'. 'She's been in a lunatic asylum for seven years Miss.'

And a second entry, for 16 November.

Most dearly loved – Just back from the Club where my life seems to centre more and more. Slightly jarred on by Winnie and Clemmie (Churchill) (who came down and sat with me while I had my supper) – talking about 'good works' – 'Good works' – my God how little they know. How *dare* they touch on my sacredest joy and call it 'good works'.

It is a little odd to me (quite apart from this and *you* and all it means to *me*) to feel so little curiosity or interest or responsibility about other people's lives as most people I know do. I can never remember not feeling it – not being haunted by the thought of the poor – and longing to do something – I suppose it is just a kink in one's temperament – perhaps a purely intellectual one. With me it is absolutely detached from any moral instinct. I am about as self-centred and as self-indulgent as it is possible for a human being to be – yet I am haunted and obsessed by the thought of the squalor and greyness and sunlessness of some lives – and by the arbitrariness with which our fates are dealt round.

Just how real those relationships at the Club became – not only to Violet but to the boys – is made clear in a a letter to Violet from Alick Carmichael, one of the Club boys, which he sent to her when she went on a journey to Egypt.

> Alick Carmichael
> Shepherdess Walk
> Hoxton
> London
> Tuesday, 18 January 1911

Dear Miss Asquith

I was pleased to receive and read your very interesting letter.

We are getting on all right at the Club and Mr Carter makes the cocoa very nice but I would like to see you at home again among us. I am glad to know you are enjoying your holiday and having hot weather. We are having a spell of London fogs at present which you know are not very pleasant.

I hope when you go on the shooting expedition on the Nile that you do not make a *nice tasty bit* for some large crocodile.

I would like, very much to see some of the sights to be seen in foreign lands which I have no doubt would appear very grand and strange to us British boys. My jersey fits me (to a tee) I have felt the benefit of it this winter and to whose kindness it is due.

The boys are getting on all right at gymnasium and our Bob thinks that some of us will be alright for the display.

You ask me if I have chosen my profession yet. I will leave the matter over till you come home. If I don't get into Mess. Brown Bros. my father would like me to learn wireless telegraphy. I will have to improve myself at night school.

Hoping you have a safe journey home feeling much better for your holiday. I remain one of your Boys.

Alick Carmichael

Then, from the diary entries for a weekend Violet spent here at Haddo, later: Saturday and Sunday 21 and 22 September 1912, when she was twenty-five years old:

My Beloved – I came up from London on Friday night. Coates brought me in some tea in the morning and there I was in real Scotch (Aberdeen scotch) country – harvest just beginning in the fields – and the September sunshine clothing everything with gold . . . We buzzed in at the Haddo lodge and up through these glorious woods – the leaves not yet changing much – the heather still out and the 40,000 rabbits scampering in every direction. I drew up in front of beloved Haddo to find them all typically assembled in front of the house being photographed! in one of those family groups we know so well . . .

Your mother and I walked down to the cemetery afterwards – in calm sunlight and sat there silently together for a little. The beech tree in front of the house on that side is so yellow one doesn't know when the sun is on it and when not. The fountain is playing and your Father constantly gives directions to higher or lower it a few inches . . .

Sunday 22 September . . . A glorious service in the chapel in the evening – held by Mr Holden – Dr Bebner preached a most touching sermon. I have never seen the chapel full before – people were sitting on chairs all the way up the aisle – and crowding outside the door. I sat between Haddo and Miss Younger in a rather tightly packed pew. The singing seemed to come out of everyone's hearts.

I would love to read that 'most touching sermon' of Dr Bebner. How did he comfort Violet and Archie's mother and father and brothers and all those others who had watched him grow up? 'We bring our years to an end, as it were a tale that is told.' Yes: that's true.

Of course, what I've said so far doesn't make a sermon. The tale I've told you this evening – very familiar I'm sure to some of you – was brought to an end nearly ninety years ago. Violet Bonham Carter's life was brought to an end in 1969; Mark Bonham Carter's in 1994.

I said at the beginning that there's no greater human gift than story-telling. But I'd want to emphasize that each of our lives is itself a story with a meaning. Archie's – Violet's – Mark's, your life and mine, are all stories that have a meaning. They couldn't have been invented by a machine or a computer.

That great mathematician and physicist, Albert Einstein, said that the most important question in life is whether God is loving. When the story of a life is brought to an end 'as it were a tale that is told', and when, particularly, that life is a young life, and someone *you* love, you are bound to ask, 'Is God – the author of the story – loving?'

The whole Christian faith depends, I would say, on our belief that when God, the Father of our Lord Jesus Christ, allowed his thirty-three year-old Son to die upon the cross he was *loving*. And, similarly, when Archie's life was brought to an end in 1909, God had not suddenly removed his love.

But there are certain reflections on the love of God we can make now. Now the death toll from motor accidents is huge compared with what it was in Archie Gordon's day. Is the motor car a gift of a loving God? And is how we handle it an aspect of that gift of love?

And now, surely, we can reflect upon the advance of medical science in the intervening years: from the ambulance service – no longer horse-drawn – to anaesthetics, antibiotics, blood transfusions, and X-rays. It is unlikely that Archie Gordon would have died from his accident today. God's love is manifested today in medical science and in other aspects of human freedom. And there is never a gift of love without the gift of freedom.

One aspect of the increase of medical knowledge relates to our human interdependence and ability to co-operate – which is also to be seen in such small things as boys' clubs or, indeed, in a school or a medical faculty, or an estate, or a village. It is part of the 'tale that is told'.

And the whole 'tale' of our life is lived against the back-cloth of Time itself, and the mystery of Time. 1909 to 1996 is a relatively long time; but it's a brief span in Time itself: which is one of God's greatest and most loving gifts, without which our lives would be meaningless. The gift of Time makes the telling of our 'tale' possible, though it may be better the subject of poets than of preachers.

I suspect that some of you may already have thought, 'Had Archie lived beyond 1909, had he lived into, say, the next volume of Violet's diaries, had he lived into 1914, would he have lived to 1918? Or would he have been one of the millions in that Great Slaughter?'

Violet's bereavement of 1909 had soon to be set against those terrible, endless lists of casualties; and many a mother and father, and many a sweetheart, had soon to learn to live with the news of a tale that had been brought to an end.

But for the Christian – it cannot be said too often – death, whenever it comes, is never the end. What form the life beyond the grave will take is a mystery, and 'now we know in part'; but, as Jesus said, 'Father, into thy hands I commend my spirit', so too can we commend ourselves and those we love into the loving hands of God, and to the 'Author of life divine'.

Last night, as I slept in the room where Archie Gordon was born, I was glad and grateful that we here could tell his tale –

and our tales – to our loving Father: the loving Author of our national, personal and family histories, indeed, the histories of our world, and of life itself.

16

Zacchaeus

Holy Trinity, Clapham; 6 October 1996

The story of Zacchaeus has been a favourite of mine from, literally, my very earliest years. I remember, across nearly seventy years now, that it was illustrated on the last page of my very first Bible Alphabet Book. There was a verse:

> Also Zacchaeus,
> who climbed up a tree
> because he was small
> and he wanted to see.

And the verse was illustrated with a huge Z, which occupied most of the page. There was a tree and its branches weaving in and out of the Z; and out of the branches, at the top, peered the very small face of Zacchaeus. And at the bottom of the tree there was Jesus, standing, and looking up to, and calling to Zacchaeus, surrounded by a crowd.

But it wasn't only my alphabet book that made me love Zacchaeus. I went to a Methodist Sunday School, and in the Kindergarten we learnt:

> Now Zacchaeus was a very little man
> And a very little man was he.
> He climbed up into a sycamore tree
> For the Saviour he wanted to see.
>
> Now when the Saviour passed that way
> He looked up into the tree.
> And said to Zacchaeus: 'Do come down
> For I'm coming to your house for tea.'

But it wasn't only my alphabet book and that lovely Sunday School verse that made me love Zacchaeus.

Later on, I well remember regularly climbing a tree, when I was about seven or eight, near St Chad's Park, Chadwell Heath, Dagenham, where I was brought up. My friends and I called it, for some unknown reason, the 'rump steak tree'. You could sit in its branches and see those who went by, without being seen yourself. You could even call out after them without their knowing where the voice was coming from. I well understood Zacchaeus' desire to hide; and I doubt whether I've ever entirely lost that desire. And little could make me love the New Testament Jesus more than this picture of the way he related to Zacchaeus.

Jesus clearly had a gift, the gift of what the poet George Herbert called 'quick-eyed love', the gift of spotting the one who wanted to hide from him – for one reason or another – perhaps for some guilt or other. But he also observed the wistfulness in Zacchaeus: the desire to receive something of what Jesus had to offer. And there was an urgency to Jesus' call to him. He made it clear he really wanted to see Zacchaeus. 'Be quick and come down,' he said. And Jesus accepted Zacchaeus in a remarkable way. He said: 'I must come and stay with you today.' Notice: it's not 'Come and stay with me'; it's 'you can do something for me'. Jesus' acceptance of Zacchaeus takes the form – paradoxically – of asking Zacchaeus to accept him. And Zacchaeus can hardly wait. He shins down the tree, to everyone's astonishment who knew him. 'He's gone home with Zacchaeus!' they say. 'He's gone in to be the guest of that sinner! – of that outsider, of that reject of our society.'

I think it's worth noting, particularly in view of what I want to say later, that that encounter of Jesus and Zacchaeus didn't take place in what I will call an ecclesiastical setting. It took place in the world at large. Jesus' ministry is a very worldly ministry. His encounter with Zacchaeus underlines that he was out and about meeting people like Zacchaeus where they were, about their daily life and vocation. And that's where

Christians have to meet the Zacchaeuses of today. But Zacchaeus today is not first other people: he's ourselves. And it's only when we've let the Zacchaeus in us meet Jesus that we can move on to the other truths that are latent within this wonderful story.

Jesus said to Zacchaeus, 'I want to come and stay at your house.'

The early church was, of course, largely a matter of house churches, not huge ecclesiastical buildings; and I expect that it made this particular story a very favourite reading in such gatherings.

There could hardly have been a better description of the early church: forgiven and accepted sinners, gathering together in the presence of the risen, forgiving, accepting Lord. The early church was a company of people like Zacchaeus: houses full of them, gathering for worship, prayer and teaching.

Perhaps its worth saying that in the 1960s, this diocese of Southwark made its name not least through its emphasis on the house church. Ernie Southcott, the Provost of the Cathedral for several years, from 1961 to 1970, had rediscovered the importance of the church that gathers in the home, in his parish of Halton, Leeds, and the church all over England had profited from his insights.

And Bishop John Robinson, Bishop of Woolwich from 1959 to 1969, added his theological weight to those perceptions of Ernie Southcott. Let me remind you of one or two things John Robinson had to say in the 1960s about the House Church.

'While the Church is always the great Church,' he wrote, 'it can be nevertheless, and must be, embodied in units which can still be described as "the church" – as it found expression at, for instance, Corinth – "the Church in your house". That small church, gathered in a house, was nevertheless the Body of Christ in its totality.'

'The theological recovery of the idea of the church in the house is one of the most important tasks of our generation,'

John Robinson wrote. 'It's a vital cell within the Body itself.'
He saw the house church saying something about the way the
church could grow and be formed. It could expand though
small cells of the Body. He also saw the house church as
saying something about the meaning of holiness: uniting the
words 'holy' and 'common': holiness and homeliness.

He saw the house church as saying something about what
we call the incarnational nature of our faith: a faith which is
literally down-to-earth. People in each other's homes could
share their work and home experience and their faith experience and could grow in Christ in a way that sometimes in
larger buildings might be prevented, or, at least might be
difficult.

John Robinson said the house church had something to say
about the true shape of Christian ministry. That ministry was
not only about bishops and dioceses or even about parishes
and priests. It needed to operate at the level of the street, and
the estate, and the house, and the office, and the works. 'The
house church movement,' I remember John Robinson saying,
'is the grass roots of the church.'

I've suggested that that phrase in the Gospel 'I want to
come and stay at your house' should make us think afresh
about Jesus and the house church. But I want to underline
what I will call the evangelical faith that must remain at its
heart. The 'Zacchaeus in us' needs to know that Jesus wants to
come to be with us, whatever our particular reason for hiding
from him.

There's a lot in this Gospel, by implication, I think, about
house communions. But Jesus makes himself known not only
in the breaking of bread but in the breaking and sharing of the
Word: where two or three are gathered together.

In our generation we have learnt a lot about what we call
'Group Dynamics'. I just want to say that the dynamics of a
house church are very different from the dynamics of a large
congregation.

But let us not entirely forget the need for places and spaces
in the church for the Zacchaeus in us to hide. There's a place

in the church for what I will call 'anonymity'. Our large churches may be like large trees. I remember once asking a well-known figure in our diocese, Dr Cecilia Goodenough, why she came to Southwark Cathedral to worship. She answered immediately 'To escape other people!' Perhaps I should add she spent most of the rest of the week with home-less people.

What I've said this morning is, of course, nothing new. It goes back, as I've said, to the early church, and, indeed, to the gospel. But each generation has to re-discover – to discover for itself – what I will purposely call 'home' truths. The truths relating to Jesus' words: 'I must come and stay with you in your house: in your home.'

I've already mentioned this morning the seventeeth-century Anglican priest-poet, George Herbert. He was very much a parish priest and, indeed, a country parson. Yet there's a poem of his which, to my mind, particularly echoes the central idea in this story of Zacchaeus: Jesus wanting to come and stay with him and have a meal with him. George Herbert wrote:

> Love bade me welcome: yet my soul drew back,
>   Guilty of dust and sin.
> But quick-ey'd Love, observing me grow slack
>   From my first entrance in,
> Drew nearer to me, sweetly questioning
>   If I'd lack'd anything.
> A guest, I answer'd, worthy to be here:
>   Love said, You shall be he.
> I, the unkind, ungrateful? Ah my dear,
>   I cannot look on thee.
> Love took my hand, and smiling did reply,
>   Who made the eyes but I?
>
> Truth Lord, but I have marr'd them: let my shame
>   Go where it doth deserve.
> And know you not, says Love, who bore the blame?
>   My dear, then I will serve.

You must sit down, says Love, and taste my meat.
    So I did sit and eat.

That marvellous poem makes it clear that the story of
Zacchaeus is not only about the house church, it's about the
here and now. It's about us who have come here to 'holy communion' this very morning: and each of us a Zacchaeus.

17

The Book of Life

Gray's Inn Chapel; Remembrance Sunday,
10 November 1996

'And I saw the dead, small and great, stand before God: and the books were opened; and another book was opened, which is the book of life.'

Revelation 20.12

Remembrance Sunday presents us each year with a considerable problem: How do we remember the virtues involved in the great wars – the courage and the sacrifice – and yet remember also the repellent and rebarbative reality of war?

To represent war in traditional words, music and art is most often to misrepresent it. Yet war catapulted artists like Paul Nash, whose work is being exhibited at this moment at the Imperial War Museum, into a sudden, unexpected and formidable maturity. The *War Requiem* of Benjamin Britten, for all its unbearable beauty, is undeniably close to the bare bones of reality. And there is poetry – like, say, some of Wilfred Owen's – which is as near perfect as human writing could ever be in articulating what he calls 'the pity of war'.

Sometimes, I walk the few hundred yards from my home to the War Museum, and simply stand in front of the American artist John Singer Sargent's 'Gassed', and stare at those blinded soldiers, each with their hands on the shoulders of the man in front, and then repeat to myself the tally of the First World War – twelve million dead; and I'm left standing in silent incredulity and revulsion. But then, as often as not, my mind returns to a simple list of names, the names of, in the main, young men, and to the individual experience of bereavement lodged at its heart. And, maybe, I think of some village shorn of so many of its youth.

Master Wellwood, of his great kindness, gave me, not long before he died, his copy of *The War Book of Gray's Inn*, published in 1921, which contains the names of the members of the Inn who served in the First World War, together with brief biographical notes on each of them. It's a book which enables you to 'see the dead, small and great', from this Inn. It helps you to think of them, individually, standing before God. But it has also made me muse upon that phrase in my text: 'the books were opened'.

The last book of the Bible, from which my text comes, is of course, a most mysterious book; and so, too, is the whole subject of what lies beyond the grave, and, indeed, beyond the end of this world. And of that we can only speak in myths and metaphors, in picture language and images. But of all the images St John the Divine uses or, indeed, might have used, the image of a book – not least because of Master Wellwood's gift – is one I find plain but powerful and accessible.

'The books were opened; and another book was opened, which is the book of life.' I imagine St John the Divine had in mind not a book that you might buy at Butterworth's, but a scroll. Yet we who still spend hours reading war histories, war biographies, war memoirs, war fiction, understand all too well that phrase 'the books were opened'.

The War Book of Gray's Inn contains also some of the speeches delivered in Hall on special occasions during the First World War. For instance, at the dinner given to Lieutenant General Jan Christian Smuts in 1917. It has the script of a sermon preached in the then Chapel on the Sunday *after* the Armistice, and the details of the service in Chapel when our War Memorial Windows were dedicated. 'I saw the dead, small and great, stand before God: and the books were opened; and another book was opened, which is the book of life.' There's nothing mythical about *The War Book of Gray's Inn*, yet such a book brings that metaphor and myth of St John within range of our understanding.

Our memorials have always somehow to face and articulate both the meaning of life and the meaninglessness of it. They have to come to terms with catastrophe. The riddle of history itself is laid bare by huge international wars. The First World War and, surely, the Second, were historical crises which posed the question of the very meaning of history, of the meaning of life. There was some talk, of course, of the crisis heralding a new day. There was facile optimism, and there was the darkest pessimism; but few, very few of us, on Remembrance Day, have no thought of the futility of it all, of what possible meaning there can be to such slaughter and such waste of life.

This morning, as we remember our European and Western carnage, out of the corner of our mind's eye, we are all conscious of what is happening in Central Africa, in terrible imitation of our genocide in Europe from time to time. It is facing such questions that has made me choose this morning my particular text: 'And I saw the dead, small and great, stand before God: and the books were opened . . .'

Recently I have been reading a most remarkable book of the First World War.

Five years ago, I took with me to Tanzania, in the steps of Bishop Trevor Huddleston, Sam Bickersteth. His father is now a retired bishop, John Bickersteth. He had been Bishop of Bath and Wells and Clerk to the Closet to Her Majesty The Queen. John Bickersteth was born in his grandparents' Canterbury home. Before becoming Canon of Canterbury, John's grandfather was vicar of Leeds. In 1915 his wife, Ella, started to keep a diary for her six sons, because one of them was in Australia at the outbreak of war. By the spring of 1915, four of her boys were on active service. She persevered with her task year after year. Eventually, it reached eighteen volumes, and more than seven thousand pages. Her diary included extracts from her sons' letters from the Front. In retirement, recently, Bishop John Bickersteth has edited the diaries, and now 'the books are opened'. What he has edited has been published, and we are presented with a deeply moving mixture of English social, military, family, and religious history.

One of the sons, Julian (later an English headmaster and canon of Canterbury) was, in fact, a chaplain in France. He had been able to get over to see another brother, Morris, fairly often, when he was not far away – a few miles along the Somme. But then came the news that Morris had been killed. As soon as he could get away, Julian rode over on his bicycle to the Divisional HQ of his brother. Here is part of his letter home to his mother:

They handed me the list of officers killed and wounded. Besides our dear Morris, Capts Neil Whittaker, Maude, Booth, Lintott, Saunders and Everett were known to be dead, whereas Vouse, Willey, James and Humphreys were missing – every other officer was wounded.

No one could give me any details, but they sent me to find a Sgt who they thought was near Morris when he fell – meanwhile they kindly took me round to their mess and gave me some food. There I met Chappell, the chaplain, almost broken-hearted over the terrible losses of the battalions. After dinner, an orderly came in and said that a private was there who could tell me of how dear Morris had died. I went out at once and found a handsome boy of eighteen, who immediately gave me all the details I so badly wanted to know. He nearly broke down several times, poor boy. He was slightly wounded and had been buried alive, but he had got out and he was the last man Morris spoke to. His name is Private Bateson, No 1218, and his home address North Street, Fryston, Castleford, Yorks. He told me that he knew Morris from the first, having been in his original platoon in 'B' Company before Morris was made Company Commander. After a terrible bombardment when the 15th lost many men, the moment came for the attack, 7.30 a.m. Saturday morning, 1 July. It was a lovely day and the sun was brilliant. Morris had been walking up and down his front line encouraging his men, and sent the

first wave over punctually to the second. He himself as
Officer Commanding the Company was to go with the 8th
wave. The first wave reached a slight rise ten to fifteen yards
from our front line trench and disappeared at that little rise.
The next wave followed, and the next, and so on, but alas!
the German lines were full of Germans with machine-guns,
and the German artillery was plastering no man's land,
which lay between the two lines, with shrapnel. Far then
from taking the first three German trenches which had been
the objective of the 15th, the brave lads never reached, or
only very, very few of them, the 1st German trench; and
all the time Morris was walking up and down the trench,
sending off each wave with a cheery word and a look of
encouragement.

The lads knew well enough what they were going out to,
but no one wavered, no one faltered and at last the time
came for Morris to go out himself with the eighth and last
wave.

'Come on, lads,' he cried, 'here's to a short life and a
gay one,' and responding to his heroic cheerfulness and
splendid example, that last wave of heroes leapt out of the
trench to face the worst. After going ten yards, they found
the remainder of the 7 and 6 platoons – only a few of whom
were left alive – lying just behind the rising ground, and the
three platoons were mixed up together for a few minutes.
Morris apparently gave the order to lie down for a moment
to try and disentangle the living from the dead, although
there were very few of the former and here it was that the
lad Bateson crawled to his side to obtain permission to go
back as he was wounded. Morris, in spite of the turmoil
and terrible fire, coolly wrote him out a chit, signed it and
told him to get back as best he could. (A 'chit' is necessary
in the case of a very slightly wounded man; otherwise he
has to stay with his unit.)

Directly after Morris handed the piece of paper to the
boy, he looked round to see if there was any support from
the trenches behind and at that moment a shrapnel bullet

struck him in the back of the head; a second later another bullet passed right through his head, coming out through his forehead. He just rolled over without a word or a sound and Bateson was able to see that he was quite dead, killed instantly. Bateson was on his left, and as dear Morris rolled over, he rolled to within two feet of him, so he was able to verify the fact that the end had come. Bateson did not leave his side until five minutes after he was struck, and he never moved or breathed again.

This excellent lad who had told me his story so simply and bravely, went on to say that seeing he couldn't do any more for his officer, he let the sergeant know that Morris had been knocked out, and so the sergeant took command and then, how he doesn't know, he managed to get back into our trench.

Immediately afterwards, a shell fell on the parapet and blew it in and he was buried, but fortunately he was dug out in time and though terribly shaken and un-nerved, he managed to get back to the Dressing Station.

Not all Julian's letters home were quite so tragic. Here is another briefer extract from one of his letters – with quite a different subject – written from near Abbeville, 25 January 1918.

There is only one job for a chaplain in France and that is with the battalion. They are the fighting men, the men who bear the brunt of war, who get wounded and recover, return to the trenches, and get wounded again until their time comes and they die. It is good to live with dying men – dying men who are in the full vigour of health and strength, whose comradeship is something past understanding, but sacred and wonderful.

These are the men who are always treated worst. They are the worst paid; they live in greater hardships; they are more away from their homes; they live in greater danger than any other man who wears the King's uniform. It is they who by their lives, their heroism and splendid unselfishness live very close to their God. They have one consolation in the midst of what most people know to be a hopeless existence, and that is their comradeship, their friendship. It is this fact alone which helps them through – the comradeship of men who have shared countless hardships and dangers together; and now even this has been taken from many of them as their little knots and gatherings of friends have been broken up and destroyed. 'Good-bye, chum, let's hope we'll meet in Blighty – some day when the war is over.' 'Keep a good heart, boy, it won't be long now.' 'Cheer up, mate, I'll write and tell you where I get to'; and many similar sayings, accompanied by hearty hand-grips and eyes brimming with tears, are heard as the various contingents formed up to march away – the majority never to meet again on this earth.

My third and final extract from Julian's letters is different again:

One short but heartfelt service was somewhat interrupted during my address by five enemy aeroplanes which came over and dropped bombs in a neighbouring field. I wanted the men to sit on the grass for the address but the colonel, who was standing ten yards in front, whispered to me that he could have no movement of any kind made by the men, so I proceeded with my address, the men remaining standing. It is always hard to talk to a standing congregation; and when the air is rent with the sound of exploding bombs at no very great distance, it is not easy to keep the men's attention. But I caught them for a moment at the end, and more so perhaps during the Blessing, having previously explained that I as God's minister was about to bless them in His Name and ask for His protection for them in 'the great endeavour'.

The German planes had moved off by the time that we had sung 'God save the King', and so the battalion was able to march off the quite open space where the parade was held without the fear of being detected. An aeroplane can never see troops if the latter remain absolutely stationery. If they move, they can be spotted at once. Every man there knew that it might well be his last service on this earth, and although the note struck was one of 'Joy', joy in self-sacrifice, joy in showing forth love which Christ Himself showed on the cross, a joy in which we are called upon to join with Him, that 'Love casting out fear' might be ours, yet there was no mistaking the solemnity of the occasion.

I myself find this book of Ella Bickersteth's diaries a 'book of life', in spite of the fact that it is so full of death.

Julian Bickersteth is so alive, and so, too, is Private Bateson. And so is that vicar's wife in Leeds: that mother of six sons, Ella Bickersteth. It is so alive with the unique and gifted creations of God's unquenchable love and life.

The whole book fills you with the conviction that Dylan Thomas expressed in six words: 'And Death shall have no dominion.'

18

The Month of Memory

November is the month of memory, which begins with All Saints' and All Souls' Days, and thus presses upon us questions like the nature of the life beyond this. Most people, when you ask them, 'What's a saint?' completely ignore the fact that originally, that's to say, in the New Testament, the word described every Christian. It simply meant those who know themselves called to participate in the holiness of God; in other words, people like you and me.

In only a couple of hundred years, the term was beginning to be restricted to those of heroic virtue who were believed to have entered directly into the company of heaven at death. Such men and women were manifestly filled with the power and holiness of God. And the cult of the saints began with the veneration of the martyrs, in the second century.

This year, for several reasons, I've been having what you might call 'second thoughts' about saints.

The first reason is that for seventeen years now I've been Director of a charity called Christian Action; but that organization, after a life of fifty years, will be closing down at the end of the year. 'Sanctity' and 'Christian action' presumably have a good deal in common I have thought. Or do they?

But alongside my years of work with Christian Action, and as Preacher here, most of you will know I've been involved in writing two biographies of leading Christians: the first, Bishop John Robinson, who was Bishop of Woolwich for ten years, from 1959 to 1969, but who died of a pancreatic tumour in 1983; and the second, Bishop Trevor Huddleston, who is aged and frail but still alive. Both their biographies, I have thought, might have something to say about sanctity; and they have.

Bishop John Robinson – who was best known as the 'Lady Chatterley Bishop' because of the part he played in the court case related to the publication of the novel by D. H. Lawrence, and as the author of the best-seller *Honest to God* – suddenly suffered such acute pain in 1983 that he knew he was seriously ill. Within days it was diagnosed as a pancreatic tumour, and he set about 'living with cancer' his last six months – to the very day.

So when, for instance, a close friend of mine, who'd been a senior scholar in law when I was Chaplain of Trinity College, Cambridge, forty years ago, but has become, in the intervening years, a Law Lord, received recently an almost identical diagnosis as John Robinson, I found I personally could do no less – and no more – than send him a copy of my biography of John Robinson, and suggest to him that he read some paragraphs from John's last sermon, which he preached in the Chapel of Trinity College, Cambridge in 1983 where he was then Dean and for which he asked me to come up to Cambridge and sit next to him, and take over if he could not get through it.

Here are just a few paragraphs from that memorable sermon:

How does one prepare for death, whether of other people or of oneself? It is something we seldom talk about these days. Obviously there is the elementary duty (urged in the Prayer Book) of making one's will and other dispositions, which is no more of a morbid occupation than taking out life-insurance. And there is the deeper level of seeking to round off one's account, of ordering one's priorities and what one wants to do in the time available. And notice such as this gives concentrates the mind wonderfully and makes one realize how much of one's time one wastes or kills. When I was told that I had six months, or perhaps nine, to live, the first reaction was naturally of shock – though I also felt liberated, because, as in limited-over cricket, at least one knew the target one had to beat (and this target was but an informed guess from the experience and resources of the medical profession, by which I had no intention of being confined). But my second reaction was: 'But six months is a long time. One can do a lot in that. How am I going to use it?'

The initial response is to give up doing things – and it certainly sifts out the inessentials. My reaction was to go through the diary cancelling engagements. But I soon realized that this was purely negative; and I remembered the remark of Geoffrey Lampe, recently Regius Professor of Divinity here at Cambridge, who showed us how anyone should die of cancer: 'I can't die: my diary is far too full!'

In fact 'preparing for death' is not the other-worldly pious exercise stamped on our minds by Victorian sentimentality, turning away from the things of earth for the things of 'heaven'. Rather, for the Christian it is preparing for 'eternal life', which means real living, more abundant life, which is, begun, continued, though not ended, *now*. And this means it is about quality of life not quantity. How long it goes on here is purely secondary. So preparing for eternity means learning to live, not just concentrating on keeping alive. It means living it *up*, becoming *more* concerned with contributing to and enjoying what matters most – giving the most to life and getting the most from it, while it is on offer. So that is why, among other things, we went to Florence, where we had never been before, and to Switzerland, to stay with friends we had to disappoint earlier because I entered hospital instead. I am giving myself too, in the limited working day I have before I tire, to all sorts of writing I want to finish. And if one goes for quality of life this may be the best way to extend its quantity. Seek first the kingdom of heaven – and who knows what shall be added? Pursue the wholeness of body, mind and spirit, and physical cure may, though not necessarily will, be a bonus.

John Robinson, as I've said, died six months to the day after the pancreatic tumour was diagnosed. Bishop Trevor Huddleston could hardly be more different from John Robinson. His raw material of holiness is, to my mind, quite different. He lives most of his life now in a wheelchair. He has been diabetic for over forty years. He has lived much of the last fifty years at the centre of some of the world's major events, but he's not particularly good at being retired now to the side-lines.

I suspect that ever since he was a child there was a kind of fire-ball of anger within him, which was very useful when that anger could be used on behalf of, say, black children, or on behalf of grown ups who were unjustly treated – like, say, Nelson Mandela when he was arrested. Holiness, in Trevor Huddleston's case, has often meant harnessing his anger to this cause and that – primarily, of course, against apartheid. And few people can have achieved more in their lifetime in the way of righting wrongs. But sometimes now there's little left but the anger. He would love to die, he says; but maybe the Lord has one or two things more for him to learn. I think growth in holiness often means asking God: 'What more do you *still* want me to learn?'

Shortly after I took on being Director of Christian Action, I was asked to write a short dictionary definition of holiness for *A Dictionary of Christian Spirituality*. Mercifully, I don't think I was meant to be an expert on anything but the theory of the subject! A few days ago, as I end my time at Christian Action, I thought I'd look at that dictionary definition again, and see whether I still stood by it. Here it is:

The holy lies at the heart of every religion and emanates from its heart. Lying at its heart, it has always an element of mystery and of the unknown, of the 'numinous', as Rudolf Otto calls it, in his great book, *The Idea of the Holy*, in which he draws attention to the fear, the wonder, the shock, and the amazement and astonishment which the holy may evoke. The holy knocks us back and draws us on.

We recognize its transcendent value. It commands our respect. It may evoke from us our best works of art and strike us dumb.

In its most primitive form, the holy has little ethical content. You touch the holy and drop dead. But in the Old Testament the ethical relation between man and the holy becomes increasingly important. Isaiah, for instance, sees the Lord, and is shattered with a sense of his own sinfulness and the sinfulness of his nation. But the vision is not simply of the holy set apart, or of a holiness which fills only the temple, but of a holiness which ultimately fills all the earth as well as heaven. And the holy calls and empowers the prophet as a servant of the holy.

People – individuals and nations – places, times, things, are called into relation to the holy. They, like the holy, are set apart, consecrated. This is the stuff of religion. The history of Israel is the history of a holy people, a people set apart. But that history is also the history of the betrayal of holiness: of holiness presumed upon; holiness as merely enjoying religious practices; holiness as an automatic status. But the call of God to holiness is followed by the judgment of God upon its betrayal. Israel has to learn that the holy requires us 'to do justly, to love mercy, and to walk humbly before God'. Holiness in the Bible reaches its climax in Jesus. He is the holy, 'fascinating', drawing all men to himself in his love and compassion; yet also the cause of wonder and astonishment, fear and trembling. The holy is revealed supremely in Jesus as self-giving love. He consecrates himself, and we 'behold his glory', in his coming amongst us as one who serves; in his washing his disciples' feet; and supremely in his laying down his life for his friends through his death on the cross.

The Christian church, the Israel of God, is God's holy people. The Holy Spirit reproduces in Christians the holiness which Jesus revealed and embodied. The ancient phrase 'holy things for holy people' speaks of the eucharist as the vehicle of the renewal of the holiness of the Christian community. Baptism – holy baptism – the Word of God – the holy Bible, prayer, all have their indispensable part in our growth into holiness and into the Communion of Saints.

It is clear that the Christian idea of the holy has very little in common with a system of taboos (the Polynesian system of prohibitions connected with things considered holy). In the Old Testament the holy is quite often forbidden ground, the God you must not look at; but the coming of Jesus radically altered that. He is the revelation of him whose 'new, best name is Love'; the revelation of the holy in a manger; a carpenter's son; crucified as a criminal. He was born and died not on days which were holy but on days which were made holy by the way he lived and died on them. He did not live in 'the holy land' but in a land made holy by the way he spent his day-to-day life there. It was from the raw material of the everyday and ordinary that he fashioned his holiness. And for ever after, for the Christian, wherever we are, whoever we are, whatever the time of day, that moment presents us in our decisions and responsibilities with the raw material out of which the holy has to be fashioned in response to God.

The holy for the Christian is therefore never simply the church, the chapel, the shrine, the sanctuary, the place set apart that a few can penetrate but which is taboo for others. It is never simply the holy day. (As George Herbert wrote: 'Seven whole days not one in seven, I will praise thee'.) It is never simply the holy man or woman – the 'sacred' ministry as distinct from everyone in their ministry. The place, time and person set apart have their function as resources for our holiness, lived primarily in the world; but they are rarely to be thought of as *the* place of holiness, and so on.

It follows that most people will have to work out their holiness through their marriage rather than through celibacy, through decisions at work as well as in the home – on boards of directors and in trades unions; in race relations and relations with the world's poor, hungry and unemployed; and with the people next door.

Holiness requires daily application. But if holiness requires us, as St Paul said, to 'work out your own salvation with fear and trembling', it requires us even more to remember and rely upon 'God who works in you, inspiring both the will and the deed . . .' The supreme witness to that is the holiness of Christ and of those whom we call his 'saints'.

Well, I don't think I want to alter or revise one jot of that dictionary definition of holiness and sanctity. But I would want to add to it now something that I've learnt not least from writing the beginnings of Trevor Huddleston's biography. God doesn't see our anger, for instance, as something that detracts from our holiness. He takes and uses it as the raw material of our holiness. Nothing is too negative to be transformed into something positive. That's what redemption, as well as sanctity and holiness, means.

My favourite of all the English saints – the Lady Julian of Norwich – said: 'He turns our wounds into worships.'

19

Messiah

Gray's Inn Chapel; Sunday before Advent,
24 November 1996

I've often said here that there are many kinds of sermon. Today, mine will simply be reflections before our 'in-house' performance of *Messiah*. Perhaps I should rather call them 'musings' before *Messiah* – not only for the sake of alliteration – for Shakespeare's use of the word 'to muse' suggests 'study in silence', with a hint of wonder and meditation.

Let's begin with where *Messiah* was first performed. There were (and are) two cathedrals in Dublin, Christ Church and St Patrick's. Christ Church is the older, St Patrick's the grander. When Handel was invited to bring *Messiah* to Dublin, Dr Charles Cobbe was Dean of Christ Church, but Swift – the inimitable Dr Jonathan Swift – was the Dean of St Patrick's, albeit half – or more than half – insane. His friend Laetitia Pilkington described him as having taken 'a wrong turn in his brain'. The Dean himself, more graphically, pointing to an expiring example, said he had become a tree 'dying at the top'.

You might have thought *Messiah* would have been first performed in a cathedral, not least because the cathedral's musicians would clearly be needed. Or, if not in one of the cathedrals, in one of Dublin's many grand churches: St Ann's, St Andrew's, St Michan's, St Werburgh's, and so on. Handel's music had already been performed in one or two of them, for charity. (The earliest performances of *Messiah* were most often for charity: chiefly for Handel's favourite interest and concern, the Foundling Hospital, now known as the Thomas Coram Foundation, which most of you will know since it lies only a short walk to the north of the Inn. Handel left the manuscript of *Messiah* to it, and gave the organ to the chapel. A visit to the Foundation, to see its paintings by artists like Hogarth, Reynolds, and Gainsborough and to learn of its continuing work, is well worth while.) The churches of Dublin might have seemed the only places large enough for the first performance of *Messiah,* and were, of course, equipped with organs. But Dean Swift had wryly written a poem to himself, in about 1730, which he called 'To Himself on Saint Cecilia's Day':

> Grave Dean of St Patrick's how comes it to pass
> That you, who know music no more than an ass,
> That you, who so lately were writing of Drapiers,
> Should lend your Cathedral to players and scrapers?
> To act such an opera once in a year,
> So offensive to ev'ry true Protestant ear,
> With trumpets and fiddles, and organs, and singing,
> Will sure the Pretender and Popery bring in.

In fact, the first performance of *Messiah* took place in a musick hall, the Fishamble Street Musick Hall in Dublin, at twelve noon on 13 April 1742.

It's unlikely to have been mere chance that Handel's visit to Dublin, and the first performance of *Messiah,* coincided with the opening of two halls purposely built for music, even if all the resources of the cathedrals and churches by way of singers and instrumentalists were nevertheless needed. But a Mr Fox, a member of one of the choirs, was probably not untypical. Swift wrote of him: 'Daily losing his voice by intemperance. Neglect in his attendance. Scandalous in conversation and behaviour.'

But there seems to me something of significance here; that *Messiah* was born, so to speak, in a musick hall: not in a cathedral or a church. A musick hall is more like a manger.

But why Dublin? – which may have been said to be 'Dublin's fair city' – in *song* (if that's not too Irish!); but it was a city of much poverty, vagrancy, disease and squalor. Beggars abounded. Dean Swift, alas, merely inveighed against them. To him they were simply 'Drunkards, Heathens and Whore-Mongers'.

Dublin, in 1750, with a population of 125,000, was the eleventh largest city in Europe: lagging, of course, far behind London, with its 676,000. Half Dublin's population – the lower half – was Catholic. The great George Berkeley, the idealist philosopher and Bishop of Cloyne, asked in 1835 'whether there be on earth any Christian or civilized people so beggarly, wretched, and destitute as the Common Irish?'

It has in fact been questioned whether Handel specifically intended *Messiah* for Dublin; but if we cannot be absolutely sure of this, there can be no doubt that Dublin received *Messiah* with rapture, and within two years began the custom of annual performance, whilst its introduction in London was by no means an unqualified success, and it was a decade before performances became annual.

One probable answer to the question 'Why was *Messiah* first performed in Dublin?' is that William Cavendish, third Duke of Devonshire, the new Lord Lieutenant and an energetic patron of the arts, asked his friend Handel to provide him with an oratorio. On such things as patronage, great music – and great musicians – then, as now, depended. The sacred still has to be paid for, often, in secular cash: 'which things are an allegory'.

And, not irrelevant, is the fact that among the many things to distinguish *Messiah* from all Handel's other oratorios, he devised it in a simple transportable form, requiring, if necessary, no more than four solo voices, and no orchestral forces beyond strings, continuo, a pair of trumpets and drums. The oboe part was inserted after Handel had composed 'Their sound is gone out into all lands' for the first London performance of 1749. Again, it's worth musing on the fact that *Messiah's* birth depended on resources: a patron and cash, as we've said, and a music hall, and, of course, a genius of a composer, and, we must add, the genius, too, of Charles Jennens in assembling the words, the rather remarkable libretto.

Charles Jennens had written to his friend Edward
Holdsworth:

> Handel says he will do nothing next Winter, but I hope I
> shall perswade him to set another Scripture Collection I
> have made for him, and perform it for his own Benefit in
> Passion Week. I hope he will lay out his whole genius and
> Skill upon it, that the Composition may excell all his former
> Compositions, as the Subject excells every other Subject.
> The Subject is *Messiah*.

In April 1742 George Frederic Handel was in his fifty-
seventh year. For the last eighteen of these he had lived in
London, at No. 25 Brook Street. For the last fifteen he had
been a naturalized citizen of Great Britain, and had made
England his home since 1713. His English was heavily
accented, and easily imitable, but, as much as German, it was
the language of his first thoughts. His home was modest for
the fashionable part of London in which it stood, convenient
for walking in the park and for worship at St George's,
Hanover Square. He had a servant, a cook, and a couple of
maids. In April 1737, however, he had suffered a stroke,
which had partially paralysed his right side, but he had made
a remarkable recovery, and his playing was but little affected.
He had written over forty operas, five English oratorios, two
German passions, and numerous sacred and secular choral
works. No other composer in Europe had even half so much
music in print.

Oratorio, as distinct from opera, raised questions for some
eighteenth-century clergy. Jonathan Swift had scruples about
the involvement of his choristers in Handel's Dublin season
of 1741–42. This was nothing new. Dr Gibson, Bishop of
London, would not grant permission for Handel's oratorio
Esther to be represented on the stage of the King's Theatre,
Haymarket, so it was performed at the Crown and Anchor
Music Club in the Strand (which some may think gives a kind
of permission and blessing to our performance of *Messiah* in
Hall!).

Richard Luckett, the Pepys Librarian of Magdalene College, Cambridge, maintains that 'Oratorio was native to Rome, with its origins in the musical entertainments which, in the sixteenth century, had formed an important part of St Philip Neri's unconventional evangelization of Renaissance Rome, and took its name from the community, the Oratory, which gathered round him.' Handel had developed the practice of performing his organ concerti between the acts of his oratorios, and had completed Twelve Grand Concerti in a month in 1739.

But let's now move a little nearer to musing on *Messiah* itself.

Right at the centre of the title page of *Messiah* is a text which is *not* set to music, I Timothy 3.16.

> *And without controversy, great is the Mystery of Godliness: God was*
> *manifested in the Flesh, justified by the Spirit, seen of angels, preached among the Gentiles, believed on in the World, received up into Glory. In whom are hid all the Treasures of Wisdom and Knowledge.*

That title-page text is clearly placed there as a kind of door through which we must needs pass if we're to understand what this oratorio called *Messiah* is all about.

It's of course a tough text, one of the most demanding in all scripture, but through that door we come to Charles Jennens' libretto, a series of direct quotations from scripture which make up a coherent and convincing whole. We come to Charles Jennens' libretto and Handel's music. So let me give you a modern translation of that difficult verse:

> *And great beyond all question is the mystery of our religion:*
> *He was manifested in flesh,*
> *vindicated in spirit,*
> *seen by angels;*
> *he was proclaimed among the nations,*

believed in throughout the world,
raised to heavenly glory.

That verse is probably an early Christian hymn or confession of faith.

No one had, in fact, ever attempted a work on the scale or of the nature of *Messiah*.

Messiah disdains narrative. It uses, with very slight modifications of detail, the language of the Authorized Version of the Bible. Those slight modifications are nevertheless significant. 'O Zion that bringest good tidings' becomes 'O thou that tellest good tidings to Zion', as in the Vulgate. A far more incisive and rhythmic phrase. 'He was despised' has been moved from the present to the past tense. 'Behold, and see if there be any sorrow like unto his sorrow' replaces 'like unto my sorrow'. And so on.

Messiah is a drama: though one in which the momentum is primarily internal. The listener's knowledge of the historical events is assumed, so that the work becomes a commentary on the nativity, the passion, the resurrection, and the ascension of Christ: a commentary and a meditation.

The word-book of *Messiah* for the London performance in the Theatre Royal, Covent Garden, of 1752 makes clear how Charles Jennens – and Handel – conceived *Messiah:* setting out with great clarity four separate acts, each like the act of an opera.

Handel, in fact, carefully records that he began Act I (or Part I) on Saturday 22 August 1741 and finished it on Friday 28 August. Part II he finished on Sunday 6 September, Part III on Saturday 12 September, and the whole work was *ausgefüllt* – 'filled up' – on 14 September: a good deal less than a month from beginning to end. At the end he inscribed *Solo Deo Gloria*.

Of course, Handel did not write down *Messiah* as if it were dictated to him. He worked away at outlines and sketches, which are of huge interest where and when they are available.

I think it's important we should muse for a while on Handel

composing *Messiah*. That scene may say something of crucial significance about who we human beings are – all of us, not just Handel. 'We are the music makers.' We need to reflect, from time to time, on the very nature of music, and the nature of inspiration, and the nature of musical appreciation, and what it has to say about the nature of our humanity. When one human being composes such a work as *Messiah* he says something about the nature of us all. He exalts us all. When we perform or appreciate *Messiah* we are saying something about who we are. 'Say it with music' is not just a 1930s signature tune, it's the signature of some of the heights and depths of our humanity. It articulates who we are better, probably, than any verbal creed. Composer, performer, listener: all say something about our humanity, and, I would say, our divinity – and yet what is composed is not detached from the time of its composition, just as Jesus was a child of his time. Incarnation is always limitation. *Messiah* is unmistakably music of the eighteenth century.

We could now go through, one by one, the actual individual solos and choruses of *Messiah*. The Reverend John Newton, the slave ship captain turned clergyman, preached and published fifty sermons on them. And, of course, there's the overture, which was an item that Jennens, who was wedded to his text, never wanted included. Handel, he said, 'retain'd his overture obstinately'. But I think today we should cease our musing on *Messiah* just as if the overture were about to begin, and the curtain were going up.

I myself find the E minor chords of the overture fill me with expectancy and awe, and even a little apprehension, at what may lie ahead, until the E minor changes dramatically to the E major of 'Comfort ye, comfort ye my people'. And then we're on to *Messiah:* to the prophet, priest, king, and saviour foreshadowed in the Old Testament: fulfilled in Jesus of Nazareth.

Perhaps I should say just this much more. Handel had to travel to Dublin by ship – no Aer Lingus then! He arrived in Dublin on 18 November 1741. He had sailed from Parkgate, on the Dee, twelve miles from Chester, rather than from

Holyhead, a sea journey of double the length, but saving sixty miles of rough Welsh roads. In fact, Handel delayed three days in Chester because of the weather, and managed to get hold of some choirmen from the cathedral to sing, at sight, something he was taking with him to Ireland, probably *Messiah*. One of them, after repeated attempts, failed so comprehensively to sing what was set before him that Handel expostulated in broken English: 'Did you not tell me you could sing at sight?' 'Yes, sir,' said the unfortunate singer, 'and so I can; but not at *first* sight.'

I like the thought not only of *Messiah's* birth in the manger of a musick hall. I like the thought of that journey to where *Messiah* would be delivered, not far from the Liffey (some call it scornfully, some lovingly, 'the niffy Liffey'). It's a journey which we all need to make afresh each Christmas to see the Glory of the Lord revealed in a manger, and we shall make our journey to Messiah this Christmas with the skilled help of our good organist and director of music Christopher Bowers-Broadbent – and George Frederic Handel.

> We too will thither
> Bend our joyful footsteps
> O come, let us adore him, Christ the Lord.

20

Kodaly's *Missa Brevis*

'Owe no man anything but to love one another': the first words of the Epistle for today – or in the New English Bible version: 'Leave no claim outstanding against you, except that of mutual love' (Romans 13.8).

That leaves, of course, a huge claim against each one of us. For, clearly, from that point of view, we're all up to our ears in debt, whether it's through failure in love in our personal relationships, or through our part in the impersonal relationships of institutions and nations. It's not only Ireland of which James Joyce could write: 'Christ and Caesar were fist in glove.' And a moment's thought makes it clear how right it is to begin any celebration of the Holy Communion, that takes seriously the restoration of communion, with those words *Kyrie eleison; Christe eleison; Kyrie eleison.*

The setting we're using today – Kodaly's *Missa Brevis* – began its life in 1942, when the Germans were attacking Stalingrad, and Rommel was in retreat in North Africa, and the Americans were struggling to recapture Guadalcanal – and Shostakovich was writing his 'Leningrad' Symphony. Kodaly meant his Mass to be a cry for mercy and for peace in the midst of a fractured and ravaged world.. His *Dona nobis pacem* at the end of the Mass is heart-felt.

In 1945 Kodaly reshaped his organ Mass for orchestra, organ, chorus and soloists. It was first performed in the make-shift concert hall where he and his wife had taken shelter. In 1945 the provisional Hungarian government under General

Miklos concluded an armistice with the Allies. You may not have existed in 1945, or, if you did, you may not have been all that aware of Hungarian history. Most of us were pre-occupied with our own bits of the Second World War. But all of us alive now know one date in 1945 that should make us say *Kyrie eleison* and *Dona nobis pacem* – 6 August 1945 – the Feast of the Transfiguration of our Lord, but also the day of the disfiguration of Hiroshima. But not only of Hiroshima, but of humanity.

Ten days ago I took part in a debate in Hall on the motion that 'This house believes religion should stay out of politics.' I was privileged to be allowed to oppose that motion.

As an incident that supported my argument, I recounted how, as a young chaplain of Trinity College, Cambridge, in the late 1950s, I sat at dinner one evening next to Otto Frisch, the Jacksonian Professor of Physics, a Fellow of the College. Frisch was a refugee from Nazi Germany. When Hitler was making speeches, Frisch said he'd kept silence. 'I'm a physicist,' he said to himself. 'I must get on with my science.' But Frisch's father was a Polish Jew. Eventually, Frisch came to England. It was while he was working in Birmingham that he did the work which proved an atomic bomb was possible. It was in 1943 that he was shipped with a few dozen scientists to Los Alamos to work on the first bomb. After the explosion of that bomb at Los Alamos Frisch said there was a lot of discussion about how to use the weapon. Should it be used at all? Should it be demonstrated on an uninhabited island? Quite a lot of people said in Los Alamos what Frisch at one time had said in Germany: 'Scientists should stick to matters of their own competence.' Frisch was now convinced that was an ostrich-like attitude. But he said to me that evening at table that he was filled with shock and dismay when he heard General Groves, the United States General in overall charge of the atomic bomb project, say to the British scientist Sir James Chadwick, who had discovered the neutron: 'You realize, of course, that the whole purpose of our working on this project is to subdue the *Russians*' – a remark which was made when the Russians were supposed to be our allies. Frisch agonized over whether he should keep silent at what he had heard or whether he should speak out.

At table that evening Frisch turned to me and asked: 'Eric, what would you have done – as a Christian?' One thing I knew I could not and must not do was to keep out of the political debate concerning nuclear weapons.

In the succeeding years I have tried to keep in it. And last year I rejoiced when I learnt that Sir Michael Atiyah, President of the Royal Society, Master of Trinity, who had been a research fellow at Trinity alongside Otto Frisch in my day, had said in his Presidential Address to the Royal Society:

I as a scientist can state my views without becoming embroiled in partisan politics, so let me venture a prediction. I believe history will show that the insistence on a UK nuclear capability was fundamentally misguided, a total waste of resources and a significant factor in our relative economic decline over the past fifty years.

From the nuclear weapons debate I do not believe any educated sensitive human being, let alone any Christian of our time, can opt out. I am proud that Christian Action, the charity I have had the privilege of leading for many years, has played a significant part in that debate, not only talking, but marching to, for instance, Aldermaston.

For a short while after the Gulf War we heard much about a new world order in which the arms trade would be severely curtailed. Alas, the rhetoric soon faded, and now, as we've heard this very week, it's 'business as usual'. But it's not enough to point a finger at the arms industry, or at the Government. We ourselves, each one of us, have to work out the meaning of love in international as well as personal relationships.

'Leave no claim outstanding against you' (says the Advent Epistle) 'except that of mutual love.'

Kyrie eleison: Christe eleison: Kyrie eleison.
Dona nobis pacem.

21

Christian Action's Final Service

St Paul's Cathedral; 7 December 1996

Some of you will be all too aware that I've already given *one* Thought for the Day, on Radio 4. That involved telling people what Christian Action has been up to in these last fifty years – in two minutes fifty seconds. You won't need to be told that. You've most of you been involved in Christian Action, some of you since its beginning. You – we – are here to give thanks.

And yet perhaps we all need to ask today very simply, 'What has been at the heart of Christian Action these fifty years?' And as soon as I do I realize I'm asking a larger question: 'What has been at the heart of Christian Action these two thousand years, that enables our work in fifty years to be called Christian Action?' And as soon as I ask that question, the answer becomes obvious.

And I can put it in the form of a story. There's a church in France with a whole window of stained glass, of several panels, each of which depicts a scene from the parable of the Good Samaritan. You can immediately tell who's the Samaritan, because in each panel he has a halo over his head. But that window contains a surprise. In one panel, it's the victim – mugged on the Jerusalem/Jericho road – who wears the halo. The glass of the window is old: but the truth it's trying to convey is older.

St Augustine said that the victim on the Jerusalem/Jericho road should speak to us of him who fell victim to Pilate, to Caiaphas, to the High Priests, to Judas, and to the people, and who suffered and died at their hands outside Jerusalem. One of Charles Wesley's hymns begins 'Victim divine, thy grace we claim . . .' You can say that the best known of all Christ's parables has two figures at the heart of it, not one: the Samaritan and the victim.

But St Augustine says rather more about this parable than I've quoted him as saying. He says that the figure lying wounded on the Jerusalem/Jericho road is Adam: man; humanity; our wounded humanity, so wonderfully created, yet also so wounded, so knocked about. But Augustine doesn't separate the Christ-figure from all this. He says Christ takes on, he embraces our wounded humanity.

This isn't just theory or theology, least of all is it simply past history. For Mother Teresa and her sisters, for instance, it has been one of their basic rules of life to recognize God in the person of the poor.

So, I would maintain, that at the heart of what Christian Action has been doing in these last fifty years is care for the victim in the name and person of Christ the victim.

If I could paint, I'd want to paint a whole series of pictures – like that window of stained glass in France – but each panel would have a different sort of victim on it: victims of the arms the nations sell to one another; victims of racial and sexual prejudice; economic victims without work, or food, or education, or a home; victims of disease – leukaemia, cancer, AIDS. And over each of them I'd paint a halo – because they, because we – are specially close to Christ.

He has taken on, embraced, accepted our wounded humanity. And his work, he has allowed us, empowered us to share; he has called us, enabled us to be involved in. His work he has said is our work; our work, his. And thus we have been bold to call it: *Christian Action*. And it's for that work that we now say: Thanks be to God!

22

The Morning Star

St Saviour's, Pimlico; 5 January 1997

Christmas is associated for us all with gifts: with presents, and, above all, with God's present to mankind: his Son, Jesus Christ. That's why we give each other gifts: to celebrate the supreme gift.

Part of the association of Christmas with gifts comes, of course, from the story of the Wise Men bringing the gifts of gold, frankincense and myrrh. And we celebrate officially, the Feast of the Epiphany, tomorrow – which is preceded tonight by Twelfth Night. This morning we're anticipating Epiphany.

But there's one other gift at Epiphany which it's important to remember, and that's the Star.

> As with gladness men of old
> Did the guiding Star behold,
> As with joy they hailed its light
> Leading onward, beaming bright,
> So, most gracious God, may we
> Evermore be led to thee.

I think it may be particularly important for you here at St Saviour's this year – without a vicar at the moment – and having your PCC meeting soon to think about your next vicar – I think it may be particularly important for you to think this year about the Star of Bethlehem: the guiding Star.

Many people these days buy a newspaper in order to see what their stars say. It seems not to matter that what different newspapers say is different! – not surprisingly! 'Must just look up me stars!' people say. 'Let's see what's in me stars!' I don't myself think there's anything more pagan – in the worst sense of that word – anything more anti-Christian – than dependence on our stars.

I know of no biblical scholar of repute who thinks that the story of the Wise Men is history, but it's a lovely legend, and a marvellous myth. And myth and legend and symbol are, of course, bearers of the most sublime truth, otherwise many of our carols could be cast away: stories of Joseph and the cherry tree, and so on.

But the symbol of the Star of Bethlehem may have a lot to say to us. What has it to say?

In the last chapter of the last book of the Bible, the Book of the Revelation, the Lord himself says: 'I am the bright and the morning star.' It's worth letting that text sink into our hearts and minds.

It means that the Star to guide us is the Lord himself, made known in Jesus. He never lets us down. He never leads us up the garden path. He will never let us down. He is transcendent wisdom and transcendent Love – and transcendent Light. But he's the God of Surprises.

I love that verse of the nineteenth-century Scottish poet George Macdonald:

> They all were looking for a king
> To slay their foes and lift them high;
> Thou cam'st a little baby thing
> That made a woman cry.

That was the surprise. The Star of Bethlehem led to a surprise.

I wonder what sort of person you are looking for as your next vicar? He will above all need to be someone who can speak to you of the God revealed in Jesus. And not only to you but to people who come here bereaved, or for their child to be baptized, or to get married. He will need to speak of the Star to guide.

'I am the bright and the morning Star.' I remember, during the Second World War, going to a play by Emlyn Williams called *The Morning Star*. It was all about the 'blitz' and the devastation and destruction of the War. But it ended with the siren sounding the All Clear, and a rather humble house-keeper, played by Gladys Henson, simply going to the window, now devoid of glass, pulling back what remained of the curtains; and looking out and up and saying – with surprise in her voice – what she saw: 'The Morning Star!' Nothing more needed to be said. And the play ends with that expression of hope and faith: 'The Morning Star'.

Here at 'St Saviour's' – not simply when you get a new vicar, but now – you as a congregation and church, through the Saviour within you, are called to be a beacon of hope in and to the neighbourhood: 'The bright and the morning star'.

In the last few years, it has been my privilege to go round the country visiting inner city parishes where the Church Urban Fund has been helping the church to relate to and serve the neighbourhood: helping young and old and people with very different needs. It's been very encouraging to me to see just what can be done. The church as a sign of Hope. St Saviour's as the Star of Bethlehem.

So:

> pray for whoever will be your new vicar;
> pray for the archdeacon and bishop;
> pray for the Church of St Saviour's;
> pray for yourself and your ministry;
> pray for this deanery and your neighbouring churches in Pimlico;
> pray hopefully, trustingly, expectantly.

The writer Evelyn Waugh says that the Wise Men asked the right questions of the wrong people, and thus provoked the Massacre of the Innocents. Before you get a new vicar, you, and those who represent you, will have to ask the right questions of the right people – archdeacons, bishops – and of each other, too. Evelyn Waugh adds that it's important to remember that the Wise Men got there in the end, and their gifts were accepted.

There's a phrase in Shakespeare's *Twelfth Night* which I love:

> Journey's end in lovers' meeting
> Every wise man's son doth know.

You and I are called to be wise men's sons and daughters. And for all of us the journey ends – this morning at the altar – in lovers' meeting.

But *the* journey – of our life – will come to an end some time. And it's worth remembering those words of Shakespeare: 'Journey's end in lovers' meeting'.

23

Farewell to Gray's Inn (i)

Gray's Inn Chapel; 2 February 1997

When I was interviewed, sixteen years ago, for the post of Dean of King's College London, the then Bishop of London, Gerald Ellison, Chairman of the College Council, and one of the dozen people interviewing me, asked me, rather aggressively: 'How is it that you who many people think of as a "radical", seem to be so happy as the Preacher to one of the most conservative bodies in the country?' I answered: 'My Lord, I have never found them more conservative than the Bench of Bishops.' I did not get the job.

In the last weeks and months, I've found myself musing as to why I have been so very happy as your Preacher, in these last nineteen years; and I thought it might be profitable today for me simply to share some of those thoughts with you.

I think that although the title you gave me is 'Preacher' – and no one can deny that preaching is a very important part of the job – neither would I deny that, for the most part, I enjoy, or, better, find deeply satisfying, the work of a preacher – the job of Preacher to Gray's Inn resembles, to my mind, much more a part-time college chaplaincy; and I loved my times as a college chaplain at Cambridge. It also resembles the job of a part-time parish priest; and I loved my time as a parish priest in south London; and after a dozen years as a Cathedral canon I was, perhaps, missing a parish.

My time as a Cambridge college chaplain taught me that a priest is not merely an evangelist and a churchman; not merely a sectarian producer of sermonettes to rally the ecclesiastical troops. A university chaplain must be concerned with truth for truth's sake; with the God of truth: the truth behind the law – and order – and disorder – and society – and science – and each individual: with the truth of divinity and humanity.

At that interview at King's there was another interviewer, Air Marshal Cameron, who was the Principal of the College. He suddenly and vigorously brandished a Christian Action Journal that I had produced and had published on *Britain and the Bomb,* and enquired whether it wasn't a little arrogant on my part to presume I knew enough about such a complex and technical subject as the nuclear question to produce and publish such a paper. I replied that I'd always been taught that the subject must never be left to the admirals and generals. As I say; I didn't get the job. But it surprised me that at an academic institution, of which I'm now proud to be a Fellow, the subject of the bomb could be dealt with so caverlierly. The people whose opinion on the subject I have valued most are people such as Sir Michael Atiyah, the present Master of Trinity College, Cambridge, and last year's President of the Royal Society; Professor Rotblat, the Nobel Prizewinner; Dr Frank Blackaby, the former Director of the Stockholm International Peace Research Institute.

I have not sought to hide from you in these last years the fact that the subject of Britain and the bomb is one which I believe no Christian in this country can avoid: certainly no Christian concerned with justice – international justice. Some of you have come back to me on the subject, which is precisely what I had hoped you might do.

When I have preached as Preacher to Gray's Inn around the country – at Llandaff, Exeter, Nottingham, Newcastle, and so on – I have preached also as someone in close touch through Christian Action with the Prison Reform Trust, which Douglas Hurd has recently joined, and as someone who has also been in close touch with prisons from within: in touch with prisoners, prison chaplains and probation officers, and in touch with the victims of crime, particularly in our inner cities. I have also felt it important to preach not simply from knowledge of the Bible, which contains such wonderful verses of scripture, such powerful instructions, as

Defend the poor and fatherless:
See that such as are in need and necessity have right:
Deliver the outcast and poor:
Save them from the hands of the ungodly.

I have felt encouraged by you to interpret these ancient texts and truths in today's setting, whatever political party I may have *seemed* to have been supporting or not supporting. And you have encouraged me also with your invitations, from time to time, to sit with you in courts at Middlesbrough, St Albans, Newcastle and elsewhere. And thus have you taught me much.

Often, my visits to prisons and prisoners have arisen not through my job here but through, say, the Archbishop's Commission on Urban Priority Areas – which took me, for instance, inside Strangeways gaol – and through my other pastoral contacts. I have seen the inside of gaols at Durham, Wakefield, Nottingham, Wellingborough and Ashbourne, visiting for sixteen years one prisoner who was an under-graduate of mine at Cambridge, a doctor who was convicted of poisoning his wife and murdering her. I have sat through two appeals against his conviction, and I still believe eventually he will be found 'Not Guilty'. Paradoxically the handling of this case has not led me to have a greatly diminished regard for British justice, but rather a greater regard for the responsi-bility and complexity of the work which is the day-to-day obligation of many of you. But I've never held a doctrine of the infallibility of the Pope or of the Judiciary. And to come here into our chapel and pray for all those who administer justice in our land has often seemed the best I could do for those in prison as well as for those who sit in judgment on them.

I have often seen it maintained in recent years, mainly by politicians, that crime and unemployment have no connec-tion. It has been my great privilege in these last nineteen years often to go from here to some town or city that is a centre

of unemployment and to meet with and listen to the unemployed. Sometimes I have been surprised just where those
centres of unemployment now are, places like Hastings and
Hove. To believe there is no connecton between crime and
unemployment would mean my going against a great deal of
my experience, and strain my credulity; and again, I have had
to testify to that in my preaching.

It was when I was a parish priest in Camberwell, just after
my time in Cambridge, that I was able to assist the Cambridge
Institute of Criminology to set up, in Camberwell, its imaginative study of juvenile delinquency under D. J. West, with
Professor Leon Radzinowicz in the background. That long-
term study continues; and its regular reports have often
assisted me in my work as your Preacher.

There is a similar, but also very different, field of experience
which has been a help to me in these years. A few weeks after
I began my work as a chaplain in Cambridge, Dr Billy Graham
came to conduct a mission to the university. I had to entertain
him to lunch. But my job after the mission was, not least, to
pick up the pieces; when people who'd given their life to the
Lord, found, shortly after the mission, that they were still
envious, still impatient, still ambitious, still passionate – and
so on.

I gave a short talk in my rooms on 'How to Receive
Forgiveness', which was published, in 1957, with a preface
by Cuthbert Bardsley, then Bishop of Coventry, and with
an introduction by Charlie Moule, the evangelical Lady
Margaret's Professor of Divinity at Cambridge. Leonard
Cutts, of Hodder's happened to be present in my rooms when
I gave the talk. He it was who suggested it should be pub-
lished; and I called it *The Double Cure*:

> Be of sin the double cure,
> Cleanse me from its guilt and power.

Simon Phipps, my good friend and fellow chaplain, later
Bishop of Lincoln, would always refer to it as 'The Treble
Chance'.

I can never be sufficiently thankful for the experience of confession, formal and informal, that booklet brought me, not only at Cambridge but in the ensuing years; the confessions of students, and of ordinands and fellow priests and of more ordinary folk. Without that experience I suspect my sermons here would have been very different. Interestingly, in the Catholic Church the Confessional is often call the 'Court of the Confessional'. The emphasis in Anglican practice is somewhat different: it is less juridical and more pastoral. I always myself look forward to the words at the end of the absolution, 'and pray for me a sinner'.

I should like to emphasize today how much you have often helped me in my work. You can't prepare people for marriage, or for their children's baptism, or visit them when death draws near or has drawn near, or serious illness, and not be yourself prepared thereby for the task of preaching.

There have been two dissimilar occupations which have engaged me personally in the last years which have nevertheless something in common and which I've no doubt have made some contribution to my preaching.

To be asked to write two biographies, and therefore to have to study and explore and concentrate on the subjects, has I'm sure considerably influenced my preaching. That one subject was a bishop and the other an archbishop has not been of primary importance. It has been the mystery of their humanity which has meant most to me.

The second occupation which has, I think, influenced my preaching has been having my portrait painted by a gifted portrait artist.

Only last Friday, I read this passage in James L. Clifford's book *Biography as an Art*:

> What, really, is a biographer? Is he merely a superior kind of journalist, or must he be an artist? Is writing a life a narrow branch of history or a form of literature? Or may it be something in between, a strange amalgam of science and art? The difference between a craftsman and an artist is

obvious. The one knows exactly what his product will be. He works with specific materials and uses traditional techniques. His skill comes as a result of serious study and long practice. The other works intuitively, evolving each move that he makes, and not certain until the end just what his work will be.

What really is a preacher – artist or craftsman? I'm not myself sure. But I think my friend, the portrait artist, Diccon Swan, taught me, without knowing it, to work more intuitively, to trust my intuitions – as he does – without neglecting or despising the craft.

Most of you have said to me from time to time: 'Have you read such and such a book? Or seen such and such a play, or film? Or exhibition? Or do you know such and such a poem?' You have often thereby prepared me to be your Preacher, and I am grateful. Poetry and preaching have so much in common. Only recently, one of you asked me if I like the poems of the Welsh poet and priest R. S. Thomas. Well, I do – very much.

How about this one: 'The Empty Church'? – which can stand for this Chapel, to which you attached me – like a ball and chain – when you appointed me your Preacher.

> They laid this stone trap
> for him, enticing him with candles,
> as though he would come like some huge moth
> out of the darkness to beat there.
> Ah, he had burned himself
> before in the human flame
> and escaped, leaving the reason
> torn. He will not come any more
>
> to our lure. Why, then, do I kneel still
> striking my prayers on a stone
> heart? Is it in hope one
> of them will ignite yet and throw
> on its illumined walls the shadow
> of someone greater than I can understand?

'The shadow of someone greater than I can understand'.

I shall always remember and be grateful for the music here in Chapel. It's the music, in particular, which has often revealed 'the shadow of someone greater than I can understand'. It's our music which has often induced in me deeper reverence and awe.

But we who call ourselves Christians do not worship an unknown God – so when I have thanked you for the way you have prepared me as your Preacher at your breakfast, tea and dinner tables, as well as alongside you at table in Hall – simply by the exchange of friendship, I will end these shared musings with another poem of R. S. Thomas that he has called 'The Musician'.

> A memory of Kreisler once:
> At some recital in this same city,
> The seats all taken, I found myself pushed
> On to the stage with a few others.
> So near that I could see the toil
> Of his face muscles, a pulse like a moth
> Fluttering under the fine skin
> And the indelible veins of his smooth brow.
>
> I could see, too, the twitching of the fingers,
> Caught temporarily in art's neurosis.
> As we sat there or warmly applauded
> This player who so beautifully suffered
> For each of us upon his instrument.
>
> So it must have been on Calvary
> In the fiercer light of the thorns' halo:
> The men standing by and that one figure,
> The hands bleeding, the mind bruised but calm,
> Making such music as lives still.
> And no one daring to interrupt
> Because it was himself that he played
> And closer than all of them the God listened.

24

Farewell to Gray's Inn (ii)

Gray's Inn Chapel; 9 February 1997

I thought I would call my sermon this morning 'A Last Sermon', not least because I so well remember my eccentric friend at Cambridge, the Reverend F. A. Simpson, preaching a sermon with that very title; and I remember no less that when he preached *again*, the Regius Professor of Divinity, the Reverend John Burnaby, approached him, brandishing a copy of the printed sermon, and saying to him with exasperation: 'Simpson: how can you preach again when you have had published a sermon entitled "A *Last* Sermon".' Simpson replied with infinite disdain: 'Burnaby: I'm surprised you do not know the meaning of the *in*definite article'.

So perhaps it's right – I have thought – that my sermon this morning should be called 'A Last Sermon'.

Last week I preached what I thought of as Part One of today's sermon. I shared with some of you some of the things which I regarded as greatly contributing to my finding the work here as your Preacher so deeply satisfying for these last nearly twenty years.

I purposely did not put into words last week what some might consider to be the all-important aspect of the work, summed up in St Paul's direct and explicit words in the first chapter of his First Letter to the Christians at Corinth, when he says 'We preach Christ crucified'.

Last week I was purposely indirect, and spoke of the way I have seen my work as Preacher associated primarily with the pastoral work involved here: the work of preparation for marriage and baptism; the work of visiting the sick, sometimes, alas, sickness to death, and visiting the bereaved: and how much I've valued the friendships established thereby. I spoke of the role of the Preacher here inescapably involving those concerned with justice: personal, national and international, and how the role of the Preacher and the poet go together, and music, and literature. But in the end – indeed, not far from the beginning – a Christian preacher has always to be able to say, not least to himself, uncompromisingly and explicitly: 'I preach Christ crucified', and to know what he means by that.

In fact, I believe that what I said last week was deeply and inseparably related to Christ crucified. Those of you who were here last Sunday may remember that I ended what I had to say with some words of the Welsh poet R. S. Thomas, a poem called 'The Musician'. On Tuesday, 18 February, most of you will know that here, in Chapel, at 6.15, there will be a performance of Haydn's *Seven Words of Christ from the Cross*, for choir and small orchestra. I shall be giving seven brief addresses, each of them on one of the Seven Words, each of them separated by the music Haydn composed in the 1780s for just such an occasion, for the Cathedral at Cadiz.

I felt that was the best way of concluding my years with you as your Preacher, and I hoped that thereby it might be clear beyond a peradventure that I had done what I could to 'preach Christ crucified'. But here at Mattins today I also want to attempt that, but by another means.

In St Paul's Second Epistle to the Corinthians, in the fourth chapter, there are some verses which sum up perfectly the role that has been mine these last privileged years. You could say Paul takes as his subject: 'Ministry and Mortality'. 'We have this treasure in earthen vessels,' he says, 'that the excellency of the power may be of God, and not of us.'

God's ministers, he says, must know themselves to be but earthenware pots: cheap, fragile, expendable, replaceable. The image would have come naturally to anyone familiar with the Old Testament. If humanity was made from the clay, indeed, from the dust, it was clear that God should be thought of as the potter. Paul contrasts the trifling value of the common earthenware pot with the treasure it contains. And if the pot is a gift of creation, how much more, he says, is the treasure within it.

Paul is talking as much of himself and to himself as to the Corinthians, or he is talking to them by letting them overhear him reflecting on himself and to himself. He goes on then to talk of the relation between suffering and ministry and the inescapable prospect of death. And he is talking to all his hearers and readers, not simply to people in some specialized ministry.

In II Corinthians 4.8 he writes:

> We are troubled on every side, yet not distressed;
> we are perplexed, but not in despair;
> persecuted, but not forsaken;
> cast down, but not destroyed;
> always bearing about in the body the dying of the
> Lord Jesus, that the life also of Jesus might be
> made manifest in the body.

It's undeniably a beautiful passage; a very remarkable and a very profound passage, which, perhaps calls for a modern translation. A recent Dominican commentator, Jerome Murphy-O'Connor (not, I imagine, an Englishman!), translates it:

> We are pressed hard, but not driven into a corner;
> despairing, but not utterly desperate;
> pursued, but not abandoned;
> thrown down, but not defeated.

Paul says that as long as he is alive he is in danger of death – that's not only *his* life, it's life. He is in peril every hour, not least from persecution; but he has been so challenged and inspired by the ministry of Jesus that he is able to talk of 'bearing about in the body the dying of the Lord Jesus'. And that makes him able to face anything that lies ahead, including, of course, death itself.

Only if we are blind fools can any of us imagine this life going on for all that long, so the centre and focus of our life dare not be wholly this life. But if we bear about in the body – our body – the dying of the Lord Jesus, the life also of Jesus is made manifest, in our words and our works. That is Paul's claim; that is his experience; that is therefore his teaching, which he passes on to us, which some of us begin to be able to confirm from our own experience.

I have many treasured moments of these last years; and I feel today something in common not only with Paul but with John, when he wrote at the end of his Gospel that 'the world itself could not contain the books that might be written'. But I confine myself today to only one recollection, which must stand for many, indeed for all.

Brian Gibbens was Treasurer here in 1984. He was the son of a Methodist minister. My memory is he was born in a manse in Madras. He had a ready sense of humour, a dry and wry sense of humour. One Sunday, after the morning service, Brian said to me quietly: 'Preacher; I do wish you'd stop using that ******** blessing.' (He added an alliterative expletive.) 'There's a phrase in it,' he said, 'I simply can't take at the moment: "Honour *all* men". I've got seven men up before me in Luton just now, and I can't honour one of them; and unless you can tell me how I can honour them, you'd better stop using that blessing.'

I did my best the next Sunday. I preached on Adolf Hitler, having that week gone through the thousand pages of John Toland's biography of Hitler, underlining in red everything that was good about Hitler. And there were a surprising number of good things to say about that terrible man. I remember Brian's comment after the sermon: 'Lost in the Court of Appeal'.

After his year as Treasurer, Brian succeeded Master Edmund Davies as Dean of Chapel, but within months leukaemia did its dreadful worst to him. And I can see him now, in St Thomas's Hospital in the slow watches of the night, not long before he died, surrounded by his wife and family. I remember he suddenly looked at me and said: 'Preacher, I'm not in charge of the moment of *severance*, am I?' 'No Brian,' I replied, 'you are not.'

'Severance'. It was such a wonderful choice of word, chosen by someone in such affliction, and under such stress. It was the perfect word to describe a moment so rarely described: a word which I doubt whether anyone but a lawyer would have ever considered using. It was the perfect word. But I doubt whether any preacher in England – indeed, in the world – would ever have heard it used; any preacher but I. These years, as I say, have been years of unique privilege that have revealed the uniqueness of individuality: the unique treasure in this earthen vessel and that.

The crucified Lord personifies the love that moves creation, that mercifully transcends creation; that love that remains when the earthen pot is shattered. The crucified Lord personifies the love that gives us the gift of that unique body that is ours and the treasure within it, and that love gathers up the fragments that remain and nothing is lost.

I preached my first sermon here way back in 1978, on 5 February. I had no idea then that I was being vetted for the post of Preacher. I preached about John Bunyan and the Pilgrim's Progress because it was in fact the 300th anniversary of the publication of *The Pilgrim's Progress* and the 350th anniversary of the birth of John Bunyan, and I was then Canon Missioner of the Diocese of St Albans, which included within its bounds Bedfordshire, where, of course, Bunyan lived most of his life.

I considered preaching this morning on Schubert – the 200th anniversary of whose birth we were keeping last week and whose *Winterreise* is a kind of Pilgrim's Progress. And there is a winter's journey in most of our lives. But we shall commemorate Schubert with his Mass in G on 2 March.

I want to end what I have to say to you this morning with a reading which happens to encapsulate and perfectly express

my faith, though it was written in the fourteenth century by a
recluse, or anchoress, who lived much of her life in a cell
attached to the Church of St Julian at Norwich. I want to read
to you from *The Revelations of Divine Love* shewed to the
Lady Julian of Norwich, which have a contentment and transcendent joy and thankfulness about them which I hope will
mark this day for us all. In the First Revelation to her, Julian
says:

> Our Lord shewed me a ghostly sight of his homely loving
> . . .
> He shewed me a little thing, the quantity of an hazel-nut,
> in the palm of my hand; and it was as round as a ball. I
> looked thereupon with the eye of my understanding, and
> thought, 'What may this be?' And it was answered gener-
> ally thus: 'It is all that is made.' I marvelled how it might
> last, for methought it might suddenly have fallen to naught
> for littleness. And I was answered in my understanding: 'It
> lasteth, and ever shall last, for that God loveth it.' And so all
> thing hath the Being by the love of God.
> Also our Lord God shewed that it is full pleasance to
> Him that a silly soul come to him nakedly and plainly and
> homely . . .

In the Sixteenth Revelation, the Lady Julian heard very clearly
the words 'Thou shalt not be overcome'.

> These words 'Thou shalt not be overcome' were said full
> clearly and full mightily for assuredness and comfort
> against all tribulations that may come. He said not: 'Thou
> shalt not be tempested, thou shalt not be travailed, thou
> shalt not be dis-eased'; but he said 'Thou shalt not be over-
> come'. God willeth that we take heed to these words, and
> that we be ever mighty in sure trust, in weal and woe. For
> he loveth and liketh us, and so willeth he that we love and
> like him and mightily trust in him; and all shall be well.

And at the very end of her Revelations Julian of Norwich writes:

Wouldst thou witten thy Lord's meaning in this thing? Wit it well: Love was his meaning. Who shewed it thee? Love. What shewed he thee? Love. Wherefore shewed it he? For Love. Hold thee therein and thou shalt witten and know more in the same. But thou shalt never know nor witten therein other thing without end. Thus was I learned that Love was our Lord's meaning.

And I saw full surely in this and in all, that ere God made us he loved us; which love was never slacked, nor ever shall be. And in this love he hath done all his works; and in this love he hath made all things profitable to us; and in this love our life is everlasting. In our making we had beginning; but the love wherein he made us was in him from without begining; in which love we have our beginning. And all this shall we see in God, without end. Which may Jesus grant us, Amen.

25

Risk

Holy Trinity, Clapham; 22 February 1997

Our subject today, at your request, is 'Risk and Christian Action'. Not the charity of that name, which we closed down last December: but the actions of Christians. Yet, I think it's important not to emphasize the distinction between truly human action and Christian action, not least because Jesus was truly human.

I want to begin by saying that we're all close to risk – and risk is close to us – by our very creation. And faith and risk go together for all of us, not just for Christians. You put your faith in someone and you risk being let down.

There's never creation without risk. There never was and there never will be: parenthood, for instance. The biggest calculated risk was creation itself, God creating a creature who could destroy himself and all the world.

There's no freedom without risk: the risk of its abuse. Hence Erich Fromm's brilliant book *Fear of Freedom*.

Independence (which is, of course, allied to freedom) involves risk. So does dependence. It involves risking the abuse of your dependence by, say, the person on whom you depend. Interdependence also has its risks. Interdependence is a kind of art and craft; but there's always a risk of it being destroyed by our desire for independence, and that's as true of nations as it is of individuals.

I think the virtues can all be related to risk. Obviously courage is very related to it. But so, too, is patience. You can risk not getting to Westminster Abbey at all if you go on patiently waiting for a 77 bus! And impatience has its risks.

'Let's get what's going at the sale while we can'; but 'what's going' turns out to be dud.

Wisdom and risk have obvious connections.

And the vices, too, can be related to risk. Fear, we've already mentioned. Foolishness, impetuosity, indiscretion, lust.

Risk can be related to going to extremes, and to extremists; but there's a risk, too, in always trying to be balanced. What a bore the person can be who is always saying 'On the one hand and on the other'. The Church of England always claims to be the middle way, the *via media,* and that is supposed to be its virtue; but it risks having both its feet planted firmly in mid air and becoming the *via mediocre.* (A mugwump was a candidate in American politics in the 1880s; but someone said 'A mugwump is a man with his mug on one side of the fence and his wump on the other'!)

Risk is related to control and the lack of it; and therefore it's related to power, and to people who have it, or seize it, or think they have it, or think they should have it, and that others shouldn't have it. There's hardly any power without risk.

Risk is related to identity: to being who you are, and being willing to display and reveal who you are. So it's related to a proper reticence to reveal who you are. Every gathering like this, every party, every meeting anyone else, involves risk. You may be shot down and trampled on. But if you don't 'come out' you risk being ignored.

Risk and pride are related: proper and improper pride. I read a book recently which I thought was marvellous. I read a review of it just after I'd finished it which said the author had been 'obscenely self-indulgent'. I bet the author was hurt. I thought he'd been courageously self-revealing.

Risk is particularly related to the Unknown. And there's a lot of the unknown to this life and this world, and to the next. 'Will we be able to make the headland by dark with this wind against us?' 'Daddy, will you catch me if I jump from this stair?'

Risk and the Unknown are related through dressing and undressing. 'You can tell what sort of person she is with that skirt on.' 'With that red silk handkerchief I bet he has his problems!'

Risk and sexuality are often related through experiment, hence part of the attraction of what we call nowadays sado-masochism – S & M.

Risk of arrest has its strange attractions, so that there's a games element in crime. When I worked at a riverside wharf on the Thames during the War, beating the police with your black market goods was one of the most popular games.

Betting and gambling underline the attraction of risk; but, of course, sport itself has a huge element of risk to much of it, not least the risk of losing. Sport makes an enjoyment and entertainment out of the risk of winning and losing.

There's a risk to every relationship: getting engaged, setting up as partners and getting married, all involve risk.

The nineteenth-century American poet Walt Whitman wrote:

Darest thou now, O Soul,
Walk out with me toward the Unknown Region
Where neither ground is for the feet nor any path to follow?

Death is the ultimate risk, and therefore the ultimate demand on faith.

Risk can be an obsession, an obsessive virtue. People may want to spend all their energies climbing, for instance, or sailing – to the detriment of their other obligations, like family.

Risking everything on one thing can either be vice or virtue: risking all on the 'Pearl of Great Price' is what Jesus commended. But no wife would commend a husband who'd risk all on something – if it's another woman! But she may commend him risking all on another job, or another house.

Risk and exploration go together: exploring yourself, exploring others, exploring the world. *Exploration into God* was the title of one of Bishop John Robinson's best books.

Both the conformist and the non-conformist take risks, different risks. Risk and invitation to others go together. 'Do you like that?' 'No, I don't.'

Risk and humour go together. Every time you crack a joke you invite a response, which may not be given. When I was a teenager there were two popular brands of cigarettes, De Reske and Kensitas. One of the first jokes which ever stimulated me at that age was of a Polish Air Force Officer saying to a girl in Piccadilly, 'Would you take De Reske?' 'No,' she said, 'I only smoke Kensitas.'

Risk and business, we all know about. And risk and possessions. And risk and insurance. And risk and politics – voting for one party and not another. And risk and responsibility. And risk and choice.

Risk and moving, to another place or another job or another house. It's the risk involved in moving which makes it such an exhausting and unsettling time: the new expenditure; the new neighbours; and new possibilities of rejection.

Risk and recital – pianists and singers know all about that. It's part of risk and public performance.

Risk and painting. I had my portrait painted by someone who lives near here. Half way through his first attempt he destroyed it. He knew it was a failure. He had a second go, following his intuitions. It was – comparatively speaking – a success.

Risk and particular jobs – like coal mining or being a test pilot – go together.

Risk and vocation – like working for the hungry in Rwanda – go together.

Cardinal Hume said to me when he came to preach at Gray's Inn, 'Eric, do you sweat when you preach?' 'Yes,' I said. 'I sweat like a pig,' he said, 'especially on occasions like this. Where can I change my shirt before lunch?' Does that go under the heading of cardinals and risk or sweating and risk? Or preaching and risk?

'Lead us not into temptation.' Isn't that about risk? Some places are more risky, more tempting than others. You go there at your peril. If you go there, be prepared. 'Being pre-pared' and risk is an important subject.

I came across this passage in a book recently: 'He risked misunderstanding of his role as an all-powerful God by wear-ing a crown of thorns and putting a towel round his waist, and washing his disciples' feet.' Christians have to follow his example of risk, each in their own way with their own gifts.

I hope I've said enough to start you talking.

First quotation:

> Better never trouble Trouble
> until Trouble troubles you;
> For you only make your trouble
> double-trouble when you do.

And, secondly, Shakespeare: *Julius Caesar*, Act IV, Scene III:

> There is a tide in the affairs of men,
> Which, taken at the flood, leads on to fortune;
> Omitted, all the voyage of their life
> Is bound in shallows and in miseries.
> On such a full sea are we now afloat
> And we must take the current when it serves
> Or lose our ventures.

That's about risk.

And, finally, the anecdote. It's about that great German Christian Dietrich Bonhoeffer and one of his pupils, who, later, became his biographer; Eberhard Bethge.

In 1940 Bonhoeffer and Bethge, were in Memel in East Prussia. They were sitting in the garden of a café when the news of the Fall of France came over the radio with a fanfare of trumpets. Immediately people jumped up and began singing the Horst Wessel song and the German national anthem. Bethge remained rooted to his chair, but he was astonished to see Bonhoeffer not only standing, but raising his arm in the Nazi salute, and lustily joining in the song. Bonhoeffer whispered to Bethge: 'Are you crazy? Put up your arm!' Later he added: 'Now we shall have to take risks for very different things – not for a mere salute.'

In a few years Bonhoeffer was dead in a concentration camp but 1940 was not the time for risk. 1940 was the time for compromise. The risk came later.

26

Schubert and the Way of the Cross

Gray's Inn Chapel; 2 March 1997

The collect for this Third Sunday in Lent from the Alternative Service Book speaks of 'walking in the way of the cross'. It's a fairly familiar metaphor: to think of our life as a journey, with each of us on a personal pilgrim's progress. And, for the Christian, that journey and the way of the cross are one.

I suppose few musicians used that metaphor of 'the journey' to greater effect than Franz Schubert, the 200th anniversary of whose birth we are celebrating this year, and whose Mass in G we are singing this morning, to play our part in that celebration.

Schubert's songs contribute most wonderfully to our understanding of life as a journey, through a landscape of, as it were, subliminal memory: the huntsman's horn, a stream, the wind in the trees, and much else besides: all take on profound spiritual significance; and nowhere is this more evident than in Schubert's last great song-cycle, the *Winterreise*: the record of a personal pilgrimage across a frozen landscape towards death. Some people only see in that superb song-cycle a testament of despair. But if it were only that, the great recordings of, for instance, Dietrich Fischer-Dieskau would surely not have such a huge sale, such undeniable popularity.

It's true that the *Winterreise* contrasts with, for instance, the joyous music of the Mass this morning; but Schubert wrote his G Major Mass in 1815, when he was only eighteen. The *Winterreise* he wrote a dozen years later, and but a year before his death, from typhus, when he was thirty-one. Yet what treasure he produced in the years between! Six hundred songs, nine symphonies – including the sublime 'Unfinished' and the Great C Major – and a huge quantity of wonderful chamber music. In 1815 alone, when he composed the Mass in G, he also composed one hundred and forty-four superb songs, eight on one day.

It's true that Schubert, at the last, leaves us with the sound of an organ-grinder, in, so to speak, 'the bleak mid-winter'. And, no doubt, he saw himself as that solitary organ-grinder, who knew no fame, nor fortune, nor lasting love. And yet that organ-grinder's music has echoed across the continents and down the centuries.

It has echoed and re-echoed because increasingly, it could be said, the music of Franz Schubert was not 'romantic', in the sense of unrealistic. There is little avoidance or denial in it. He seems to say, at the end: 'Life is like this. Life is the way of the cross as I have described it in my music.'

Schubert does not attempt to turn winter into spring or summer. He offers his way of the cross, portrayed in music, as company and sympathy for others who tread the same way.

I do not myself believe we should simply contrast the warmth of the Mass in G with the cold of the *Winterreise*. Two hundred years on, Schubert's music lives in a way that Schubert himself would never have dared to hope or believe – not least because he did not romanticize the way of the cross. He 'told it as it is' – as he himself walked that road and carried his cross.

The Mass in G, the 'Unfinished' Symphony, his songs, all his music, with a growing profundity, helps us to walk the way of the cross. Today, let us give thanks for the God-given gifts of Franz Schubert, and for the help Franz Schubert gives us as we tread the next steps on our way of the cross.

For the Christian – thanks be to God – the way of the cross is not the whole of the story. And, with Schubert's music to help us, we can pray:

Almighty God,
whose most dear Son went not up to joy
    but first he suffered pain.
and entered not into glory before he was crucified,
mercifully grant that we,
walking in the way of the cross,
may find it none other than the way of life and peace,
through Jesus Christ our Lord.

27

The Song at the Scaffold

St Peter's, Vauxhall; Passion Sunday,
18 March 1997

We often speak of the 'story' of the cross: the 'story' of the Passion. But I'm not sure we always realize what a wonderful story it is, and how many other wonderful stories have stemmed from it. I'm not sure we realize that we need stories to give meaning to our life, and, in the end, we need the story of the cross more than any other. And each year Passiontide gives us the opportunity to hear and receive the story again: the story that is summed up in the last words of the Gospel for today: 'And when I am lifted up from the earth, I shall draw all men to myself.' This morning, I want to tell you just one of the stories that have stemmed from the story of the cross.

I'm going to begin the story 'Once upon a time . . .', though this story begins, in fact, at the time of the French Revolution, and takes place in France. The central character of the story is Blanche de la Force, and the story begins with her birth – or, rather, it begins with her mother, her aristocratic mother, expecting her birth, travelling home in her carriage, when, for whatever reason, the carriage was overturned. The horses panicked. Rumour had it that Blanche de la Force was born in the half-wrecked carriage. But that was not true. Her mother was confined prematurely, and died soon afterwards. Blanche survived, but only just, the circumstances of her birth.

Not only superstitious people, but also qualified physicians later associated the temperament of Blanche with her birth. She was a fearful child from her first days – fearful if a dog barked, or at the sight of a snail, fearful always that something near her would collapse on her. It was no use explaining there was no cause for alarm. Her proud name – de la Force – was a mockery.

Her father, the Marquis de la Force, engaged an excellent governess to look after her. He himself was an unbeliever, but realized from the first that Blanche, unlike himself, had profound needs of a religious nature. She was by no means unintelligent, and her governess saw to her religious instruction with diligence. So it was not altogether surprising that, after the passage of years, the governess had to inform the Marquis that Blanche had no desire to marry. What she wanted above everything was to become a nun. The Marquis, of course, at first objected, but soon realized his objections would be in vain.

Blanche was immediately happy in the Carmel de Compiègne. That does not mean that all her fears were at an end. Soon after her entrance into the nunnery the Prioress died. Her death struggle was painful beyond words, and for long hours that part of the convent where she lay dying – which was the part where Blanche had her cell – was rent with her cries of agonizing pain. Blanche was bewildered and shocked, and asked why God permitted so holy a daughter of his to suffer such pain, and began to fear her own death.

But this was not her most immediate fear. In the year 1789 the National Assembly was taking action against all religious orders, to relieve the financial pressures on the state. Blanche dreaded the death of her convent even more than her own death, because it was clearly so close at hand. When Blanche, because of the approaching secular forces, was hurriedly admitted as a postulant into the order, she was given the name of Blanche of the Agony in the Garden.

Blanche was, as we've said, not without intelligence. Some of her questions were profound. One day she asked the Reverend Mother: 'Must fear and horror always be evil? Is it not possible they may be sometimes deeper than courage? Is there not virtue in something which is so close to reality: to the terrifying powers of the world – and indeed to the reality of our own weakness and vulnerability?' One of the sisters was scandalized by the very question. 'Poor child,' she said, 'she has come to the convent like a bird seeking a nest. We should have made it clear she will not find it here. This is a place for strong souls. It is certainly no place for waverers.' Meanwhile Blanche, who had shuddered a little when she heard the name that was to be given her, prayed daily: 'O Lord Jesus, in this Garden of Gethsemane, I give myself with you, alongside you, for you and to you.'

It was not long before the agents of the government made their presence known in the neighbourhood. When they arrived at the convent, they soon went from cell to cell interrogating abrasively each of the nuns. Most of them withstood the questioning with boldness and courage. Blanche was so terror stricken she could not utter a word. Indeed, she flew to the arms of her novice mistress, so that her interrogator, an uncouth, humourless sort of fellow, gave a guffaw. He quickly turned his attention to the Reverend Mother, and asked her: did she not fear what the forces of the state had it in their power to achieve? 'How can we fear anything but the thought of displeasing Christ,' she replied: 'Christ, whom you are giving us the honour to proclaim.' When the interrogator departed, the Reverend Mother said to the nuns that she felt 'a tall solemn funeral taper had been lit within her and was bright with light'.

But Blanche was at the end of her tether. Nowadays we would describe her condition as one of near breakdown. She accused herself endlessly of weakness and failure, and begged the forgiveness of the sisters and for their prayers that she should be able to set a stronger example; but she showed her real self in anxiously enquiring again and again where the latest robbery of a convent had taken place.

Reverend Mother went on exhorting her sisters. 'Now is the great hour of the Carmelite Order,' she said. The soldiers were not long in coming, but, before they arrived, one of the sisters had left the convent like a frightened rabbit. They noticed, of course, when one morning Blanche was not at communion; but it was after Mass that they realized she had fled. They were dismayed, but not surprised.

It was the very next day that the sisters were led into the cobbled square of Compiègne. The crowd had gathered before the town hall. They marvelled to see the sisters: their bodies more upright than the soldiers, as they were led to the steps of the scaffold. The crowd stood still at first and for a long time there was virtual silence, save for the soldiers' boots on the cobbles and the sound of them shouting their orders.

Suddenly there was the sound of a single voice singing, a frail, quavering, treble voice singing: 'Veni Creator Spiritus. Come, Holy Ghost, our souls inspire.' As suddenly, the whole crowd took up the sound, full and clear. It was the voice of Blanche of the Agony in the Garden that had begun the singing and inspired every other voice in the crowd. And as the last of the nuns ascended the scaffold it was Blanche who came to join them. There was little sign of courage or defiance about her as she approached the final sacrifice. She looked at best a reluctant, almost unintentional victim.

I've told you this story this morning for several reasons. I read it first when it was first published in English in 1953 as *The Song at the Scaffold*. It was given me when I was still a curate in Westminster by the person who had been my Dean at King's College, London, Eric Abbott, who was later Dean of Westminster. It has been a very influential book in my life and ministry.

It was published first in German, in 1938, by the German novelist Gertrud von le Fort. She called it *The Last on the Scaffold*. She had found the story in another book. What she had found was a true story, or a story with a good deal of truth in it. In 1947 the French novelist Georges Bernanos set about turning the novel into a film, but it turned out that he had only a few weeks to live. Nevertheless, the story meant a great deal to him as he faced his own death. Later, the English actor Robert Speaight organized a reading of what had come to be called *The Dialogues of the Carmelites*, and in 1957 Francis

Poulenc used these 'dialogues' for the libretto of his opera of that name, which some of you may have seen and heard.

I said when I began that this is a story which stemmed from the story of the cross. I tell it you this Passion Sunday to lead you back this year to the story of the cross.

28

Easter Bereavement and Easter Joy

St Paul's, Knightsbridge; Third Sunday after Easter,
20 April 1997

At Easter, almost every priest, and a good many lay people, are aware of two emotions – indeed, two convictions – that contrast but should not conflict.

On the one hand, Easter is characterized by such a phrase as began our first hymn this morning: 'This joyful Eastertide'. Today's liturgy had as its introductory sentence: 'Jesus appeared to his disciples at the sea of Tiberias after he had risen from the dead. Alleluia!': and there's the alternative sentence: 'Jesus said, I am the resurrection and the life. Alleluia!' These phrases characterize the first emotion and conviction.

But there's a second Easter characteristic. Every priest and preacher is well aware that many come specially to church at Eastertide, bearing with them the memory of a recent bereavement.

I can't myself remember an Easter when I did not come to church with someone on my mind who'd recently been bereaved, or, indeed, having myself been recently bereaved by the death of a close friend or relative. And I always feel an obligation to preach at Easter to what we nowadays call this 'double agenda'.

This year was no exception. I was conducting the Holy Week and Easter at Tewkesbury Abbey.

On Easter Day I had in mind a friend, John, who happened to be a judge whom I had got to know through my work amongst lawyers in Gray's Inn. After retirement, he and his wife took a well-earned holiday; but on holiday, alas, his wife died.

'What should I say to John this "joyful Eastertide"?' I thought. What does Easter say to him, and to others as bereaved as he is bound to be?

In fact, ever since Easter my phone at home seems not to have stopped ringing with the news of unexpected deaths.

Norah, the widow of a priest who was a very close friend of mine before either of us was ordained. She was buried last Thursday.

Richard, a fellow theological student with me at King's College, London, who eventually became the Anglican Bishop of Argentina and Uruguay. He was buried yesterday.

Most tragic of all: John, aged 48, who was Secretary of the Archbishop's Commission on Urban Priority Areas. I spoke to him on the phone in hospital only eight days ago. Now I have to preach at his funeral at St Albans next Thursday.

What should I say this joyful Eastertide to his wife, to his children and aged mother? He was an only boy.

This is all the second aspect of the Easter agenda.

Well, of course, I have no easy words for the bereaved: no 'quick fix'. The gospel isn't like that.

The gospel isn't only the isolated story – the isolated stories – of the resurrection. And, in fact, much of what I would want to say to John, the judge – after listening to him, for as long as he wanted to talk – would be what I had to say from the pulpit during the Three Hours of Good Friday. For, surely, one has first to establish – maybe re-establish – against all appearances, that God is Love, and has such people as John and his wife in his care. That would mean saying a good deal about how Jesus revealed the nature of God in his earthly life, and supremely in his death on Calvary.

As Bishop Walsham How's hymn, 'It is a thing most wonderful' says:

But even could I see him die,
   I could but see a little part
Of that great love, which, like a fire,
   Is always burning in his heart.

But I also find myself most often asking people who've been bereaved what it was they most loved about the person whom they loved but see no longer, because it's important to spell out the gifts God has given to us in those we love, which are part of what counters any idea that God is merely cruel and arbitrary. Often what we call these days our 'bereavement anger' is our anger that we have had removed from us – at least for the moment – a person whose gifts were to us so valued and valuable. Our grief is great because the gifts were great: God's gifts in them, and to us through them, are great.

'Rolling away the stone' – the stone of bereavement – 'huge as it is', begins, I believe, not on Easter Day itself, but with everything that confirms for us the reality and nature of God's love. We are all of us created for death: created for death by the God of love, whose love will still have us in his care when this life is over. Jesus revealed God as unimaginable love, and told us that he has prepared for us 'such good things as pass our understanding'.

The resurrection is above all the sign and symbol of that Love which will not let death have or be the last word. Love is the first and last word.

The stone rolled away is the sign and symbol of that love which we have seen revealed not least in the lives of those we love, but revealed most chiefly in Jesus: in his life, and death, and triumphant suffering.

Of course, as St Paul said: 'Now we see in a glass, darkly', or 'Now we see puzzling reflections – enigmas is the Greek word – in a mirror.' 'Now we know in part.' But now – here and now – we see daffodils and blossoms, that are not to be despised as signs and tokens of God's love in creation and redemption.

The hymn that I most want to quote at Eastertide, to those

who are bereaved and to those who are facing death, is not 'officially' an Easter hymn. It's by the seventeenth-century Puritan Divine, Richard Baxter. He wrote:

> Christ leads me through no darker rooms
>   Than He went through before:
> He that unto God's Kingdom comes
>   Must enter by this door.

> My knowledge of that life is small
>   The eye of faith is dim;
> But 'tis enough that Christ knows all
>   And I shall be with him.

There my sermon today might end; but I want to add just a brief 'PS'.

In 1950, when I was a theological student at King's College, London, living in Vincent Square, Westminster, and just before being ordained as a curate to St Stephen's, Rochester Row, in this deanery, a marvellous painting of the resurrection by Veronese was bought for the chapel of the Westminster Hospital, then in Page Street, Westminster. It was bought by Christopher Hildyard, who had been a minor canon of Westminster Abbey since 1932, but had also acted as one of the chaplains to the Westminster Hospital.

Many a time when I was a curate, and had to visit someone in the hospital, I would go to the chapel, and sit or kneel before that Veronese painting; and the resurrection power of Christ would seem to flow from that sixteenth-century painting. I particularly remember a six-year-old child with leukaemia, Alastair Hetherington. I met with several nurses for prayer in the chapel while Bishop Cuthbert Bardsley laid hands on Alastair in the ward. Recently, that painting has been cleaned and restored, and has been replaced in the new Chelsea and Westminster Hospital in the Fulham Road, and new detail has been revealed in the painting.

I have preached to you this morning about the need for the

resurrection and the crucifixion to be held together, both manifestations of the Love of God in Christ.

In that Veronese painting you will see what I mean. The action of the painting is at night. It's as though the artist wanted us to be fully aware of the darkness that surrounded the resurrection – the darkness that surrounded and followed the crucifixion – in which the Love of God was made manifest: the darkness not least of bereavement. It is the heroic love of Christ which causes Christ to rise effortlessly, as it were, from the tomb. He dramatically strides upwards. His pink cloak, banner, accompanying angels, and radiant aureole around him, all speak of his Easter triumph.

This joyful Eastertide includes all our bereavements and rises from alongside and amongst them. Alleluia!

May I suggest that this Eastertide you try to make your own personal pilgrimage to that hospital chapel in the Fulham Road, and ask to be filled with resurrection life, and to be a bearer of that life to all who are bereaved.

29

Goldsmiths and Stewardship

St Vedast-alias-Foster; Annual Service of the
Worshipful Company of Goldsmiths, 21 May 1997

'If I have made gold my hope, or have said to the fine gold,
Thou art my confidence;
If I rejoiced because my wealth was great, and because mine hand
    had gotten much;
If I beheld the sun when it shined, or the moon walking in bright-
    ness;
And my heart hath been secretly enticed, or my mouth hath kissed
    my hand:
This also were an iniquity to be punished by the judge;
for I should have denied the God that is above.'

Job 31.24–28

'And he called him, and said unto him, How is it that I hear this of
thee? Give an account of thy stewardship; for thou mayest be no
longer steward.'

Luke 16.2

I count it a great privilege to respond to your Prime Warden's
kind invitation that I should preach to you this evening at this
your Annual Service. He gave more than a broad hint that it
would be particularly pleasing to him were I to take as the
subject of my sermon 'Stewardship', and quoted some words
from *The Lord of the Rings* which are inscribed on his
Goldsmith's drinking goblet: 'For I too am a steward. Did you
not learn?'

I'm more than happy to accede to the Prime Warden's
suggestion, but I have to say that the parable of the Unjust or
Unfaithful or Dishonest Steward bristles with difficulties,
some textual, some ethical, which over the centuries have

given rise to a welter of conjectural explanation; and I do not propose to detain you this evening with the minutiae of interpretation of that particular parable; I would rather confront the broad subject the Prime Warden has set before us; but I shall endeavour to keep what I say close to that marvellous question which is embedded in the parable at its very beginning: 'Give an account of thy stewardship; for thou mayest be no longer steward.'

We are most of us strangers, I think; so let me first say an introductory word or two on how the subject of stewardship has confronted me.

After spending seven war-time years working at a riverside wharf on the Thames, from the age of fourteen to twenty-one, I went to night-school at King's College, London, did a degree, and, in 1951, got ordained to a curacy in Westminster. After four years I became chaplain of Trinity College, Cambridge, and entered a world which was at first foreign to me but which has radically altered the rest of my life. When I arrived, there were nearly a thousand members of the college, senior and junior. I stayed for four years, with about three hundred new members each year. So I collected, willy-nilly, a galaxy of friends and acquaintances. That was 1955–1959. Forty years on, I am thankful to say, many of those friendships still persist, and provide me with much of the material from which I come to any tentative conclusions on the subject of stewardship.

A week or so ago, for instance, I received a package of papers from Theodore. He read English and Theology at Trinity. On his mother's side he's a direct descendant of the Randlords, the Beits, Otto and Alfred. He is therefore as rich as Croesus. As soon as he left Trinity he bought up a newspaper, *The Central Africa Examiner*. He has spent most of his life in Zambia, as, I've no doubt, a steward.

About the same time I heard from Gavin, who inherited a huge brewing business on his twenty-first birthday. I conducted his marriage forty years ago this year, while he was still at Trinity. Next month I shall gladly join in the celebration of that occasion. Brewing and stewardship, of course, raise some quite complex questions. Gavin and I have often gone together to 'case' a new hotel his group had purchased.

Most weeks I manage to see one or two erstwhile Trinity men – now judges, or foreign correspondents, or doctors, or what have you. Part of my stewardship, while doing other jobs, like running an inner city parish, has been to try to keep my friendships in repair.

The phrase from the scriptures that I most like to describe my own job – calling – profession – comes from our lesson today: 'Stewards of the mysteries of God'. It's a huge privilege to baptize the babies of one's friends after marrying them; to talk over with them – if they ask – their problems; to visit them in sickness, and, alas, all too often now, after forty years, to conduct their funerals.

But I don't think that phrase 'stewards of the mysteries of God' should be reserved only for those of us who are ordained. Each of us, surely, by our very creation, is a steward of the mysteries of God. And, of course, the mystery of iniquity, of evil, is as mysterious, and all but as powerful, as the mystery of good, and of God.

There's one curious incident I should like to recount to you as a comment on the subject of stewardship.

In the early 1970s I was asked by the then chaplain of University College, Oxford, David Burgess, now vicar of St Lawrence Jewry, to preach on a Shrove Tuesday evening. I sat at dinner next to the Master, Lord Redcliffe-Maud. My eyes wandered down the table to a marvellous Coldstream portrait of Sir William Beveridge. I turned to the Master and said: 'Master, I've just finished reading Beveridge's autobiography. In the very first paragraph he says: "I have seldom been without influence; I have seldom had power." He makes it clear he's never wanted power. The sub-title of his autobiography, he says, might be Virgil's phrase "*Sic vos non nobis*: Thus do you, not for yourselves".' The Master smiled – quizzically, I thought. He was one of Beveridge's successors, as Master. 'You know why he said that?' he asked. 'No,' I replied, and waited for his comment. 'Beveridge only had influence,' he said. 'He never had power; but he desperately wanted it.'

I have never myself, as a priest, had power, except the power of influence. But that power I have always seen as a very important part of stewardship.

In more recent years I've taken to writing one or two biographies. Biographies, it seems to me, inescapably 'give an account' of stewardship. I read them voraciously, but write them only with fear and trepidation.

The biography which has enthralled me most in recent months has been Antony Thomas' biography of Rhodes, subtitled *The Race for Africa*. It's a book which I think has much to say to us all about stewardship, not least about the stewardship of gold.

The television series, based on the book, has been rightly called by one reviewer 'a course television yarn'; but the book is intelligent, detailed, subtle, well-researched and historically sensitive. I recommend it, without reserve, to everyone.

The great South African novelist, Nadine Gordimer, reviewing the book, wrote: 'This is a true story of our times, and all times, splendidly told. For even one who has no interest either in Africa or Cecil Rhodes will find this book a remarkable achievement, because its theme is no less than universal: a mystery of the human personality. How is it that an individual who has visionary genius and energy, which could be a great source of human progress, becomes corrupted by this resource itself and turns to evil manipulation of others' lives, betraying, so to speak, himself? In Cecil Rhodes, colonialism is flamboyantly personified, and with it the awful charisma of power. Antony Thomas explores the man's amazing life with lively intelligence, scrupulously fair and informed insight, and a deep understanding of the influence on the subsequent history of Southern Africa this rogue-adventurer, romantic mining Midas, statesman, racist, hero of imperialism has had.'

You will understand that I cannot just pass over the fact that Rhodes was the son of a clergyman. He was born in 1853, the fifth son of Francis Rhodes, vicar of Bishop's Stortford, the fifth of nine children. At fifteen, Cecil wanted to be either a barrister or a parson. There's little in the records of his childhood to tell us for certain what kind of man he would be, and sons of the clergy are not always either godly or happy; but we might have hoped that in such a childhood Rhodes would have learnt the elements of Christian stewardship. Alas, at sixteen, Cecil fell ill. His lungs were said to be affected, and the vicar and the family doctor decided a long sea voyage would be the best cure.

My own brother, also a priest, asked me only a week or so ago, when he was in hospital: 'Would you agree, Eric, that the most important things in your life have happened not because of your own choice?' I did not answer immediately, but I thought of Rhodes' sea voyage and illness, and how that determined his stewardship would be located largely in Africa. He called his lungs his 'skeleton in the cupboard'.

We know that the last night the young Rhodes was in England, he spent at a concert in the Royal Albert Hall. His biographer tells us he sat next to a Mrs Bennett. She could not recall the programme, but remembered that the music had been very moving, because the young man sitting next to her suddenly burst into tears. His sobs soon became so loud that he started to attract attention, so she leaned across and tried to calm him. After the concert the young man apologised for his behaviour and explained that the next day he was sailing for Africa, the doctors having told him that a sea voyage was his only chance of life. His heart was heavy at leaving England and the music had been too much for him. The Bennetts invited him back to their hotel and asked his name. It was, of course, Cecil Rhodes. That picture is significantly different from many, if not most pictures of Rhodes we are given.

I cannot attempt even a potted biography of Rhodes this evening; the biography is there for you to read, but there are some salient features of the biography which clearly raise questions about stewardship.

Rhodes left £100,000 to his old college, Oriel, and, of

course, the provision of a scholarship fund that has done much to perpetuate his name and memory and continue his contribution to the world. That was a most significant act of stewardship.

It would be easy to forget the fact that in 1873, when he was twenty, Rhodes returned to England, matriculated to Oxford, and visited and revisited his university until he graduated in 1881.

Few biographies, if any, have made me think more about the very nature of human corruption than Antony Thomas' *Rhodes*.

When, fifty years ago, I was a theological student, my Dean of College at King's College, London, Eric Abbott, who was my close friend as well as my mentor, made an aside to me one day which I barely understood at the time. 'Eric,' he said, 'you're a romantic; and unless you have a high doctrine of corruption, you'll not survive.' As I say, at the time I barely understood him; but I did realize he was instructing me to take seriously our human capacity for corruption, though he added, I remember, that the Christian's doctrine of glory and faith in the possibility of human redemption must always be as high as his doctrine of corruption. In fact, I had to wait twenty-five years before certain personal experiences within the church brought home to me the meaning and truth of those words.

Reading the biography of Rhodes, I found, extended my understanding of human corruption. Let me quote from a review of *Rhodes* by John Carlin in *The Independent*.

He beat his rivals not by fighting them but by seducing them. By bribery (Rhodes coined the expression 'every man has his price') or sheer force of personality or, more often, both, he submitted members of the British cabinet, Kruger's Boers and proud African chieftains to his will.

Such were his powers of persuasion that after a smallpox epidemic struck Kimberley in 1883, he prevailed upon local doctors to sign false documents declaring the outbreak to be a rare skin disease. Thus did he prevent the temporary closure of his diamond mines and thus did at least 751 people needlessly, hideously die.

His biographer's thesis is that the most lasting and most evil legacy Rhodes bequeathed was, in fact, the system of apartheid itself.

Reading a biography that is in large part a history of British 'empire-building' in Africa one is struck by the similarity there often is with the rise of Naziism. Years before the rise of fascism, Rhodes professed his belief in the superiority of the white race. Hitler, decades later, said Britain had been foolish not to take Rhodes more seriously . The corruption of racial arrogance is insidious, and, of course, runs counter to the concept of stewardship. It was Rhodes' corruption which Hitler most needed to take seriously, but not only Rhodes' corruption. Rhodes was the evil genius of a society rank with greed, arrogance and cynicism.

Corruption is penetrating and pervasive. Ultimately and tragically it can be all-pervasive, devouring nations and races as well as individuals; but most often there are remarkable surviving traces of good and of God, even in the most unjust and corrupt stewards. There is, for instance, in the life of Rhodes one notable incident which, to do him justice, must be told: a time when he bravely wore the badge of courage. It forms, in fact, one of the finest passages in Thomas' biography of Rhodes. It narrates how Rhodes quelled a bloody uprising by the Matabeles after venturing entirely unarmed into the bush to negotiate with the rebel tribesmen. There, not only the potential of Rhodes was displayed, but the reality of his greatness, that was also so often squandered and misdirected.

Two final points in what must necessarily be a sermon that does but skim the surface of a large and complex subject.

As a young man, his biographer tells us, Rhodes had a strong religious sense. He believed (or needed to believe) in a power beyond himself and in purposes transcending mere money-making. The answer did not seem to Rhodes to lie in

Christianity. 'Modern research,' Rhodes wrote, 'had pulverized the authority of the Bible' and, besides, he had already experienced enough in the diamond fields to cause him to question the Christian faith. In a letter to his brother Frank, Rhodes concluded a moving description of the slow death of a friend ('he died by inches') with the observation that 'one's belief in anything to come gets very weak out here when, as you know, nearly every mortal is an atheist, or next to it'.

Does the concept of stewardship in the end depend on having a lively Christian faith, or at least a lively sense of the existence of God, and of the image of God in every man? I suspect it does.

Finally – and it's a word I carefully choose and use – Rhodes was understandably conscious all his life of its brevity: of his vulnerability and mortality. His famous last words were said to be: 'So little done. So much to do.' Was it his constant consciousness of the precariousness of his existence that pathologically fed his greed and lust for power? 'Expansion is everything,' he said. 'I would annex the planets if I could.' Rhodes was always a young man in a hurry. He was only forty-eight when he died. It was as though the words 'Thou mayest be no longer steward' were always ringing in his ears, and shaped or distorted his stewardship.

When I consulted the *New Dictionary of Christian Ethics* on 'Stewardship' I found it said: '*See* Energy; Environmental Ethics; Image of God'. Each of those terms has something to say about Rhodes and how he regarded the stewardship that was his, but each of those terms also has something surely to say to us and about our stewardship.

I have found in Rhodes' biography no neat quotation to end a sermon on stewardship to Goldsmiths. Rather, I find myself wondering whether Rhodes ever read William Blake, and, if he did, what he made of him. Did he, I wonder, ever ponder Blake's words:

> The Door of Death is made of Gold
> That Mortal Eyes cannot behold;

But, when the Mortal Eyes are clos'd,
And cold and pale the Limbs repos'd,
The Soul awakes; and wond'ring, sees
In her mild Hand the golden Key:
The Grave is Heaven's golden Gate
And rich and poor around it wait.

30

Fr Gerard CR (Geoffrey Beaumont): 'He Died Merrily'

St John's, Waterloo; 1 June 1997

Our local parish magazine reminded us this month that 'A church is part and parcel of the community in which it is set, and at St John's, Waterloo, we are aware of our links with those who live or work here and those who travel in for entertainment. This year's Festival,' it said, 'is for the whole of Waterloo.'

I suspect that here at St John's you would also include in your community those who have had some past associations with St John's. Our past is always inescapably part of us. We don't need a psychiatrist or a historian to tell us that. Each of us knows it to be true. So I gladly come here tonight, to preach during your Festival, not only as a near neighbour from Kennington: I come here as one of those who can thankfully remember – and has, indeed, been visiting St John's – for over fifty years.

And whenever I come to St John's I think thankfully of one person in particular: Fr Geoffrey Beaumont, who was here as a curate exactly fifty years ago. He was in fact here eight years: from 1934 to 1941, and from 1946 to 1947. I was present when his Requiem was celebrated here nearly thirty years ago by Bishop Trevor Huddleston, then Bishop of Stepney.

I first met Geoffrey in this neighbourhood during the war, by which time he was a chaplain to the Royal Marines, and I was working at a riverside wharf on the Thames between Southwark and Blackfriars Bridges, the very site where the

Globe Theatre has just opened. That was before I was ordained. A friend of mine, an ordinand who had joined up, to whom Geoffrey was chaplain in the Royal Marines, said that I simply must meet Geoffrey. I made an appointment to see him at his lodgings in 1 Addington Street (now all but destroyed) at the west end of York Road, when he came on leave. Characteristically, Geoffrey didn't turn up. So I took myself off to a pub, to the Waterman's Arms, which was on the site where the Festival Hall now stands. Before ever I got into the pub, I heard the sound of music, of a pub piano and singing. It was, I discovered, Geoffrey playing the piano – in his cassock – surrounded by Southern Railway porters, male and female, singing at the tops of their voices. (Female railway porters were a war-time innovation.) There was a pint pot on the top of the piano.

Geoffrey was wonderful at getting alongside ordinary working people, though he was just as good with public school types, having himself been at Cheltenham College.

When he came back from the war, he came back here, just for a year. Then he went up to Cambridge, to be for five years chaplain of Trinity College, where I would be chaplain a few years later. Geoffrey made his mark on everyone, academics and ordinary undergraduates. Rumour has it that he kept a keg of gin by his bed, but the people who spread the rumour were not least those whom he prepared for confirmation. What is certain is that he somehow made the most unlikely people interested in religion or, rather, in God. While he was at Cambridge, he wrote quite a lot of Noel Coward-type light music for the Footlights revues, which he'd also written when he was here. (Here he used to get up an annual pantomime, and edited a rather arty-crafty parish magazine.)

After being at Trinity College, Cambridge, Geoffrey spent four years as chaplain to the British Embassy at Madrid, and made many friends of toreadors! A Church of England priest who could make friends of Roman Catholic, Spanish bull-fighters is a rare bird indeed!

Then Geoffrey returned to South London, to be vicar of St

George's Camberwell, another so-called 'Waterloo' Church, virtually identical with this one, with the same architect, Francis Bedford, and built at the same time – 1824.

In Camberwell, Geoffrey returned to his unique and remarkable ministry in and through pubs. He went from one pub to another, playing the piano, singing with a cigarette in his mouth, and getting alongside people, young as well as old. It was not always what I will call a 'sober' ministry. It was a 'syncopated' ministry – he went unsteadily from bar to bar. Geoffrey's voice had to be heard to be believed! Years of smoking had given him a gravelly voice and a cough that was unforgettable!

It was while Geoffrey was at Camberwell that his Folk Mass, which brought coach-loads of people to St George's, hit the headlines, and Geoffrey became one of the leading lights of the Twentieth Century Light Music Group, which published several of his hymn tunes. The one for 'Now Thank We All Our God' we shall sing at the end of the service.

Geoffrey only stayed at St George's, Camberwell a couple of years. The simple truth is that he was hopeless at administration, though he had marvellous other gifts. To follow him as vicar, as I did, was to learn just how many people were devoted to him. The young churchwarden I inherited would say he owed a very great deal to Geoffrey. When I got to St George's I found the iron railings around the church had been taken away during the war for scrap metal, but they were very necessary to the security of the church. It was not long before I found a railing-maker who wanted to make the railings in memory of Geoffrey, whom he had only met in a pub.

I had followed Geoffrey at Trinity College, Cambridge, a few years after he left there, and I remember his coming up to Cambridge early in 1959, to say to me that he couldn't go on any longer in Camberwell. He knew that being a vicar was just not for him. I said: 'You must go round and see Mervyn Stockwood' – who had just been appointed Bishop of Southwark. 'He'll have more time to talk with you now than he will ever have when he becomes bishop.' Geoffrey returned from seeing Mervyn Stockwood and said: 'Mervyn says he is happy for me to leave St George's – on one condition.' 'What's that?' I asked. 'On condition that you take my place there!' So, for a second time, I found myself succeeding Geoffrey.

I have to say that Geoffrey's Folk Mass was not an entirely unmixed blessing to me as his successor at Camberwell. The congregation was divided into those who loved and those who loathed it. To end the division, we decided to give no warning when it was 'Folk Mass Day'. But when we had the Folk Mass, as soon as it started up, one of the anti-brigade fainted, with hysterics!

Geoffrey had, in fact, decided that he must test his vocation as a monk at Mirfield, the Community of the Resurrection, in Yorkshire. He was the oldest novice they ever accepted, but he was blissfully happy there, under his new name of Fr Gerard.

Geoffrey would often come down and stay with me when he wanted a few days in London. He told me a story of his days as a novice which I can never forget. I'd asked him what he most hated as a novice. 'Oh, I can tell you that straight away,' he said. 'It was a Beach Mission on the sand at Felixstowe.' He couldn't bear it, because people on holiday in their 'deck chairs' were 'got at' by the preacher, a Mirfield 'Father'. And there were lots of callow students to help the preacher – or that was the theory. Geoffrey simply had to stand around, in the crowd, in his cassock, after he'd helped gather the crowd for the preacher from their deck chairs. He did – until, to his joy, he saw a notice which said: 'Bathing Costumes for Hire'. That did it! He slipped quietly away and hired one – 1950s model, black, with shoulder straps. He got into it, and rejoined the crowd. A few minutes later, one of the students, not now recognizing Geoffrey without his cassock and glasses, pursued him. 'Have you been saved?' she tenderly enquired. 'Saved?' he said. 'I've not been in yet.'

That story is really a parable. You can't be saved in this world unless you've been in it: part of it. That story underlines another characteristic of Geoffrey – his humour. (He claimed to have preached for the Architects' Association on 'All the foundations are out of course'.)

Geoffrey was eventually sent out to the Community of the Resurrection's House at Stellenbosch in South Africa. He dreaded going out there and spent his last evening in England with me, dreadfully depressed. He thought the South African Boers would be the opposite of the kind of people he got on with. But in fact he was immediately happy there. He soon sent me a telegram which simply said: 'It's just like Madrid.'

Geoffrey died in Stellenbosch on 24 August 1970. I happened to be on holiday in France with Simon Phipps, my fellow chaplain at Cambridge, later Bishop of Lincoln, who had also known Geoffrey well at Cambridge. I went to the railway station at Perpignan to buy an English newspaper. In it, I saw the news of Geoffrey's death. It said three words: 'He died merrily.' There was only one thing for Simon and me to do – to have a drink in his memory!

When I visited South Africa only a few years ago I was glad to have to go to Stellenbosch. Outside the church was Geoffrey's grave, with those three words: 'He died merrily.'

As I say, his Requiem was held here nearly thirty years ago. I remember it well, not least because a little boy served Bishop Trevor Huddleston; and just before the Bishop gave the blessing the back door opened – that's to say, the front door of the church – and a man came in and shouted from the back to the boy at the altar: 'Come home Albert, your Mother ain't given you permission to be out late.' Bishop Huddleston smiled and said: 'If he'd said "Come home Geoffrey", I need not have said any more' – and then gave the Blessing.

I've told you about Geoffrey this evening, because it's your Festival, and because Geoffrey was a very special person; a very special Christian, a very special servant of God, a very special priest and a very special member of St John's Waterloo – part of your past which has been such a blessing to this part of God's world.

'Some there be that have no memorial.' I'd like to see a

memorial to Fr Geoffrey in South London. Let me be more direct: I'd like to see one here in St John's. Some would say his Folk Mass and hymns are his memorial. Certain it is that those who knew him will never forget him.

31

'The Place where the Cloud Settled'

Emmanuel Church, West Hampstead; Centenary of the Laying of the Foundation Stone, 19 June 1997

'Whenever the cloud lifted from the tent, the Israelites struck camp, and at the place where the cloud settled, there they pitched their camp.'

Numbers 9.17

It seems to me important this evening that we should face fundamentals fairly speedily. And there is nothing more fundamental than the mysterious presence of God – or should I say, the presence of the mysterious God – in the cloud that settles, so to speak, over every church and congregation; and for a hundred years now has settled over this place and people. As we sang in John Newton's great hymn: 'Glorious things of thee are spoken':

> Round each habitation hovering
> See the cloud and fire appear
> For a glory and a covering
> Showing that the Lord is near.

The mysterious God, in my experience, manifests himself through three further mysteries: the mystery of place; the mystery of time; and the mystery of people. Let us this evening look briefly at each of those three mysteries.

The mystery of place: your choir has appropriately – and beautifully – sung this evening Anton Bruckner's 'Locus Iste'. I've no doubt there are many who bless God and who have blessed God for this place. You'll know, I expect, Kipling's lines:

God gave all men all earth to love
But since our hearts are small
Ordained for each one spot should prove
Beloved over all . . .

Kipling was, of course, writing of Sussex-by-the-sea. But I've
no doubt it's just as true of West Hampstead. We are all of us
people of particular places. Chesterton said: 'For anything to
be real it must be local.' A foundation stone is an anchor – an
anchor and an anchor-hold – for the ark of the church in a
particular place. It locates us in the otherwise overwhelming
mystery of space. And because of that anchor all sorts of
ministry takes place in a particular locality. People will bless
God because here, at this sacred space, they were married;
here, they or their children were baptized; here, they were
schooled; here, they were supported in their sickness; here, at
the death of loved ones they found faith in the life that transcends death. And in all these the voice from the cloud spoke
in this particular place. Here, week by week, the Word of God
has been ministered and the Sacrament of Christ's Body and
Blood. Here, in this place 'where the cloud settled'.

There's a sense in which the mystery of place is the most
easily grasped. A foundation stone is solid. A particular building is literally tangible. But the second mystery – of time – is
so much of the stuff of our very existence that all too often
we simply take it for granted. What is time? We measure it:
with seconds, and minutes, and hours, and days, and months,
and years and centuries. We clock it up, literally. But what is
it?

It takes a Shakespeare to spell out the mystery of time. He
speaks of the 'abysm of time'; 'devouring time'; the 'bank and
shoal of time'. 'O call back yesterday' – he says, on such an
occasion as this – 'bid Time return.' Shakespeare set us the
example of constantly musing and meditating on the mystery
of time, yet never being satisfied that he'd plumbed that
mystery: 'Time will come and take my love away,' he said.
Shakespeare fashioned a hundred and more other marvellous

phrases, yet never was satisfied he'd captured the mystery of time.

If this centenary were to make us aware again of the mystery of God through the mystery of time, that would make this centennial celebration of memorable worth. 'Whenever the cloud settled . . .' it settled at a particular time.

But there's a third mystery through which the voice from the cloud speaks to us: the mystery of people, particular people.

When your vicar wrote inviting me to preach today, he sent me some informative literature including a history of the church and I was delighted to recognize several names mentioned. I am old enough to remember Prebendary E. N. Sharpe who ended his days, I believe, as Archdeacon Sharpe. I see Dr Walford Davies drew up the specification of the 'new' organ at the turn of the century. As a boy I so well remember the voice of Walford Davies, by then Master of the King's Musick. I remember his programme 'Music and the Ordinary Listener' first broadcast in 1926 but which went on each week for a dozen or so years. I hurried home from school to hear him. I notice that the great Harold Darke was your organist from 1906–1911. I heard him give recitals during the early days of the Second World War at St Michael's, Cornhill. But each person in your history – named or unnamed – was and is a mystery: a wonderful and sacred mystery. And, believe it or not, you are a wonderful and sacred mystery, and will, of course, think of people you have known whose memory you treasure.

I have spoken of God made manifest in the mysteries of place and time and people. But, of course, at the heart of the life of the church wherever it is to be found is the revelation of the mystery of God in the person of Jesus Christ. In *Choruses from 'The Rock'* T. S. Eliot so marvellously speaks of that event:

Then came, at a predetermined moment, a moment
  in time and of time,

> A moment not out of time, but in time, in what we call
>   history; transecting, bisecting the world of time,
>   a moment in time but not like a moment of time,
> A moment in time but time was made through
>   that moment: for without the meaning there is no
>   time, and that moment of time gave the meaning.

That moment of time, Anno Domini; that place, Bethlehem; that person, Emmanuel, God with us – gave the meaning to our lives, and gave the meaning to all the ministry which has emanated from this church since its foundation stone was laid. Emmanuel, God with us, gave the meaning to this church.

And let us be clear that a most important part of Christian faith and life is, by focussing on one place as sacred, to remind us of the sanctity of all God's earth; and, by focussing on a particular moment in time, to remind us of the sanctity of every moment; and, by focussing on the sanctity of Jesus, to remind us of the sanctity and divinity of every human being. And that has implications for everyone in West Hampstead – for everyone in God's world, rich and poor, and of whatever race.

By your kind invitation I join you tonight in thanksgiving for this church. I join you wondering at the mystery of God which lies behind all our lives, and, above all, at the mystery of Jesus Christ Our Lord, who revealed with greatest clarity the God who is revealed in each one of us, churchgoers or non-churchgoers. who inhabit this particular part of God's earth. I join you in being thankful for this place 'where the cloud settled'.

32

'Whoever will be Great . . .'

The Chapel Royal; The Feast of St James,
27 July 1997

The Gospel that is appointed for the Feast of St James the
Apostle – for, that is, the Patronal Festival of this Chapel
Royal – could hardly be more appropriate.

It begins with the mother of Zebedee's children – by name,
probably, Salome; probably a sister of Jesus' mother: in other
words 'family' – close family – with in her mind, therefore,
what she regards as a justifiable desire for her sons to be
accorded some precedence. She comes to Jesus, we're told,
'worshipping him' – that's to say, giving him the respect which
she thinks is his due – but then saying: 'Grant that these my
two sons may sit on your right hand and on your left . . .' That
simple word 'grant' – notes Dr A. H. McNeile, in his highly
revered commentary – is a word of 'royal command'.

Here, surely, in the week of a royal garden party, it's not
difficult for us to imagine the sort of scene and situation the
Gospel describes. 'Grant that my two sons may sit the one on
thy right hand and the other on thy left . . .'

It's a very natural request of a mother, proud of her two
sons, for them to be given position and place and precedence.
How infinitely understandable, surely, in a royal court. I suspect some Under Secretary or Gold Stick in Waiting could say
immediately to us: 'Yes, it reminds me of old so-and-so.'

It's tempting for some, of course, to use this passage simply
to have a crack at the whole concept of hierarchy. However,
in my experience, hierarchy never really disappears, not even
in Trades Unions, or, indeed the Mothers' Union. But I cannot

myself ever imagine the Mother of our Lord wrangling over her position. She was too conscious that, whatever she was, she was because 'he hath regarded the lowliness of his hand-maiden . . .'

It's one of the remarkable things about monarchy that, paradoxically, the anointed figure of the monarch does not deserve to be royal. He – or she – is what he or she is wholly by the accident of birth, or, we Christians would say, by the vocation of birth.

And it's that thought, surely, that prepares us for Jesus' further words in this so appropriate Gospel for this festival and this chapel. Jesus says, and in so saying lifts the whole subject to another level: 'Ye know not what ye ask. Are ye able to drink of the cup that I shall drink of?' It's as though he said: 'You are interested in place and precedence and position? You shall have it. But have you considered what it involves? Position brings responsibility. Exaltation has its cost, even its suffering, and its sacrifice. And there's a hierarchy not only of rank but of calling and self-sacrifice.'

It was a subject that Jesus had already been facing – wrestling with – probably in the wilderness. And he knew he would have to go on facing it to the end, the very end. Born to power and to position. Yes, you will be lifted up – but on a cross.

And then Jesus takes this seminal and profound thought even further. He says 'The Gentiles' – which in those days would undoubtedly have included the occupying power, the Romans – have princes who 'exercise dominion'. 'They that are great exercise authority upon them. But it shall not be so among you; whoever will be great among you, let him be your minister. And whosoever will be chief among you, let him be your servant.'

I've already emphasized that this is an eminently appropriate Gospel. I should also say it's a tough Gospel. It means that for a Christian court and a Christian country *Servire est regnare*. To serve is to reign.

It is, I know, important for preachers in this Chapel to

eschew sycophancy, especially royal sycophancy. But, whatever views we may have on the future of the monarchy in this
country, there can be few who would question that our Queen
has over the years given us a remarkable example of dutiful
service.

Again: this country has surely been fortunate that its armed
forces have been called 'the Services'; and this role and title
have become increasingly important. Their work in places like
Bosnia – and Northern Ireland – underlines that.

And may I say that it has been important to me personally,
from a child, that the Prince of Wales, and the Princes of
Wales before him, have had as their motto 'Ich dien': I serve.

We live undeniably in a land of privilege: not least the privilege that the Christian gospel has made its ineradicable mark
on our society, so that Christ's call to service is heard and
answered by many, though they may no longer accept the
name 'Christian'. Christ's call to service is understood to lie at
the heart of the life of our nation, however much that call is
ignored or forgotten, and needs from time to time, and in each
generation, to be given fresh understanding, fresh interpretation and fresh dedication.

For the last ten years and more I have been privileged to see
a great deal of the inner cities of our land, through the work
and report of the Archbishop's Commission on Urban Priority
Areas. I have been privileged to meet with the unemployed in
many of the great cities of our land.

I would have to say – and say unhesitatingly, but very
thankfully – that much of the most perceptive and profound
response to that situation has been shown by the Prince's
Trust. No organization has done more to inspire and assist the
most disadvantaged young people both to develop themselves
and to serve the community.

I have to say – on this particular day and in this particular
place – that I would hope that everyone in the congregation of
this chapel would feel a very special obligation to be in close
touch with the work of the Prince's Trust – to be familiar with
and spread its message; maybe to volunteer time to help the

Trust; maybe to give it financial support, and perhaps to involve the place where you work. Everyone can help the Trust in some way. It's a marvellous thing, surely, that our new government has such an organization to turn to as an example, as a partner, and as a pioneer of much of what it knows it has now to do.

I believe, in short, that it must be a matter of profound thanksgiving that the Prince's Trust has given us all an immediate, practical and down-to-earth way of responding to our Lord's words in the Gospel. 'Ich dien' should not only be the Prince's motto, but ours.

'The princes of the Gentiles exercise dominion over them, and they that are great exercise authority upon them. But it shall not be so among you; but whosoever will be great among you, let him be your minister. And whosoever will be chief among you, let him be your servant.'

33

St Bartholomew and Jan Struther

St Stephen's, Rochester Row; The Feast of St Bartholomew, 24 August 1997

It's a great delight to come again to preach at St Stephen's, where I was a curate forty or so years ago, and preached most of my first sermons.

I wonder how many of you, if any, remember a film that was a huge box-office success in the middle of the war: *Mrs Miniver*. My memory is that Greer Garson and Walter Pidgeon starred in it. I don't remember much now of the film itself. It was about an English housewife in a typically rural part of England – in Kent or Sussex – and how she survives the war. I can remember she was particularly proud of a hat she'd just bought. I also remember her husband suddenly going off to France, in a small boat, to rescue some of the soldiers marooned on the beaches of Dunkirk.

I very clearly remember, too, the end of the film: the local vicar preaching a sermon in their bombed church. Now, I suspect, I'd be embarrassed by the sermon; and, probably, by much of the film: by its sentiment, its false sentiment.

But I remember that film for the power of its story. And I remember my mother getting the book out of the local library, as the book was also a best-seller. And I remember the author was someone who called herself Jan Struther.

I say 'called herself', because Jan Struther was not the real name of the author. That was just a pseudonym. Her real name was Mrs Joyce Anstruther Piaczek. She died when she was relatively young, in 1953 when I was here as a curate.

Jan Struther wrote, under that name, articles for *The*

Times. She wrote several short stories and novels; she had a book of her poems published, and she wrote several hymns, a dozen of which were published in a hymn book that became very popular in the 1920s: *Songs of Praise*, edited by Percy Dearmer. One of her best-loved hymns, 'Lord of all hopefulness', we shall sing later on: but she wrote a hymn for today – that's to say, for the Feast of St Bartholomew, which you'll also find in *Songs of Praise*.

I think she knew she had a difficult task in writing that hymn, because, the fact is, we know little or nothing about St Bartholomew except that he was an apostle. Sometimes he's identified with Nathanael, in St John's Gospel. And that may have drawn Jan Struther to him, who, as I've said, herself used a pseudonym – and drawn her to try her hand at writing a hymn about Bartholomew whose name simply means 'Son of Tolmai'.

Let me read that hymn of Jan Struther to you now.

O Saint of summer, what can we sing for you?
How can we praise you, what can we bring for you?
Lost are your words, your deeds are nameless,
Saint without history, mute and fameless.

Said you wise sayings? No one has hoarded them.
Worked you great wonders? None has recorded them.
Only your name, time's hand defying,
Shines with the light of your faith undying.

So fade the words, so vanish the deeds from us
Of each lost summer, swift as it speeds from us;
We jest, we toil, we weep, but after
Slip from our memories grief and laughter.

Only the sun that cheered us and shone for us,
All else forgotten, ever lives on for us;
Kindling our hearts when summer's ended -
Soul of the summer, serene and splendid.

Time, take our words and do what thou wilt with them;
Death, take our hands and all that we built with them;
Only our faith, our soul's endeavour,
Take it, Lord, make it, Lord, shine for ever.

Maybe Jan Struther was drawn to St Bartholomew for another reason. As a novelist, as the author of *Mrs Miniver*, she would have known how important stories are to us all; and she would have known that behind every name there's a story: that to everyone there's a story which hardly any other person knows, or knows fully.

Whenever I return to St Stephen's, invariably – and understandably – my mind immediately fills with memories: partly with stories; but almost all those stories centre on people – the vicar and the other curates, and the parish worker, the churchwardens, and members of the congregation.

Many of the people I know have long since moved away, and many have now passed away. What I know is that behind each name I remember there's a story.

Miss Colvin, whom I used to lunch with almost every Sunday, and who sat, bolt upright, always with her hat on, shrouded in black, at the end of the table. She was in her nineties, and looked exactly like Queen Victoria. Colonel Godfrey, who ran an antique and gift shop off Leicester Square, where all the curates who committed matrimony bought their engagement rings.

And there were the people I prepared for confirmation. David Hemmings, who became a doctor and went off to Canada. Alastair Macdonald, a young engineer, who went off to Sri Lanka and other parts of the world, building reservoirs. Each person I think of has a story. Each of you – each of us – has a story, a valuable story.

But I want to distinguish between two types of story. *Mrs Miniver* was purposely a story about an ordinary, middle-class person. I think Bartholomew – Saint Bartholomew, the Apostle Bartholomew – would also have wanted us to listen to what I will call 'the story of his soul': how he encountered

Jesus and the difference that made to him. Each of us could also tell the story of our soul.

Pope John XXIII, who died in 1963, who was, in many ways, a very simple person, and delighted in 'making complicated things simple'; who led the whole church into new life through the Second Vatican Council, kept a kind of diary which, when he died, was published, as *The Journal of a Soul*. It was really the story of his encounter with God, and an example to us all, how, from time to time, we ought to reflect on the story of our soul.

A book came out recently called *The Well Within: Parables for Living and Dying*. It's by Simon Bailey. In his introduction, he describes how the book came to be written. In 1985, just before he was inducted to his first parish of Dinnington, in the Diocese of Sheffield, he discovered he was HIV Positive, the virus of which often leads to AIDS. While he was fit and well he kept this fact almost completely to himself, but when he began to become visibly ill, he realized that he had to face this uncomfortable, unexplored secret, and to find ways of speaking out of his experience of 'living in the face of dying' – not least to his congregation. One of the ways that he found of doing this was by telling stories, stories reflecting his own journey. It was as his illness developed that the stories collected in his book came to him.

Simon recognizes that for some people, confronting a life-threatening illness leads simply to an enduring panic, but that for him it was as if unnecessary clutter had been removed from his life. He speaks of the attempt to be as openly and simply honest as possible, with no pretence, and he reflects on 'the burden of secrecy' as a huge extra burden 'alongside the virus itself'.

He says that he is not one of those who, living with AIDS, has come to say 'it was the best thing that happened to me'; but he still wants to speak of there being something of grace about living in the face of dying. The stories express a clear sense of the beauty and gift of life. Speaking of his new awareness of different people – family, friends, parishioners, people who have shown they care – he says: 'Relationships remind me more than anything else that there is no time to waste, life is precious, beautiful, to be celebrated, lived intensely, with honesty and integrity.' Simon died in 1995. His book, although begun late, is the story of his soul.

Mrs Miniver; St Bartholomew, our story. The story of your soul – my soul: John XXIII's, Simon Bailey's. A story that will have an ending sooner or later. The beginning of the story is God. The end of it is God.

Let me just read the poem by Jan Struther that we will soon be singing as a hymn:

Lord of all hopefulness, Lord of all joy,
Whose trust, ever child-like, no cares could destroy,
Be there at our waking, and give us, we pray,
Your bliss in our hearts, Lord, at the break of the day.

Lord of all eagerness, Lord of all faith,
Whose strong hands were skilled at the plane and the lathe,
Be there at our labours, and give us, we pray,
Your strength in our hearts, Lord, at the noon of the day.

Lord of all kindliness, Lord of all grace,
Your hands swift to welcome, your arms to embrace,
Be there at our homing, and give us, we pray,
Your love in our hearts, Lord, at the eve of the day.

Lord of all gentleness, Lord of all calm,
Whose voice is contentment, whose presence is balm,
Be there at our sleeping, and give us, we pray
Your peace in our hearts, Lord, at the end of the day.

34

In Memoriam: Princess Diana

Southwark Cathedral; 7 September 1997

I count it a great honour and privilege to respond to the
Bishop's invitation to preach at this service, the official service
in the diocese of Southwark in memory of Diana, Princess of
Wales.

Last Sunday, early in the morning, I had to scrap the
sermon I'd prepared for St Saviour's, Pimlico, just across
Vauxhall Bridge, because of the tragic news of the death of the
Princess, earlier that morning. I'd heard the news of the accident in the middle of the night; then there was still hope – at
least for the Princess; by seven, the tragic truth had been
revealed.

What I want to do this afternoon, is simply to reflect with
you on what this momentous week has to say to a diocese: to
the cathedral, and to the parishes and people of Southwark.
It will, I'm afraid, sound more like a shopping list than a
sermon.

First: this week will, I think, have surprised many in our
nation who've not counted themselves 'religious', but who,
confronted by death and tragedy, and the extinguishing of a
young and vital life, have surprised within themselves a need –
indeed, a hunger – to come to terms with the events; and have
done so with flowers, and candles, and a kind of pilgrimage to
Buckingham Palace, or Kensington Palace; and, finally, by
giving their rapt attention to a service – not in 'any old place'
– but in a church, indeed, in Westminster Abbey.

And all that, I believe, says something about our so-called
'secular' age; and about the ministry of the church; and, today,

about the church in this diocese in particular. There are clearly still times in the lives of most people – inner city, suburban, upper crust – when they have a profound need of what the church can provide, however unused to it they may be, and whatever demands it may make upon us to be flexible, and sensitive, and imaginative, to what in fact they need – which is, in the end, no different from what we ourselves need.

Secondly: those of us who call ourselves 'Christians' must surely be very thankful at such a time for what we believe, however questioning our faith, and however frail our hold on it may be – and however much this last week has caused us to think again about just what we do believe, and why. But without a profound faith, how does one confront the death of one so young and vital as Princess Diana? And how does one face the future?

Thirdly: people this week have been praying in a way that many will not have prayed for quite a while, praying for the Princess and for her sons. Untutored prayer it may often have been; but some such words as 'Lord, have mercy' have been the spontaneous prayer on people's hearts, and often, indeed, on their lips. It is for such a place as this cathedral, and every church in the diocese, to take hold afresh of its vocation to be a sensitive and imaginative centre of faith and prayer: a place which patiently endeavours to turn untutored prayer into the kind of prayer which our Lord himself taught us to pray; a centre of faith and prayer for the young, the teenagers, the middle aged and the elderly. But let us be thankful for the example the Princess has set us of listening to the young, to the minorities, and to the non-establishment groups. Let us be thankful for the appeal of her uninhibited humanity.

Fourthly: the death of Dodi Al Fayed, a Muslim, has meant this week a new outgoing towards people of other religions, an instinctive and natural realization that God is the God of all humankind. It need not weaken our Christian faith to see God at work in many and, maybe, unexpected guises. The God who has created us all in his image is not without witness in us all. And he is – to use Gerard Hughes' great phrase – 'The

God of Surprises'. This cathedral church has been here since
the twelfth century, before the tragic division between
Catholic and Protestant. But in our global village today, when
so many of different races perforce move across the face of the
earth, there needs to be a new charity in Christians – not least,
of the Church of England; a new hospitality; a new searching
for the work of the Holy Spirit in people of very different
backgrounds and cultures from ourselves. And, seeking, we
shall find.

Fifthly: Princess Diana was, of course – as her brother said
yesterday at her funeral service – a very complex person. So,
too, is the Prince of Wales. So, too, are we all. But something
has come across to many of us this week, not least through
television: something of the giftedness of Princess Diana.
People have wanted to respond to it and recognize it. But gifts
are just that. They are gifts. Gifts come from a giver. We
watched and wondered at the gifts of the Princess, as, for
instance, she bent over a sick child; touched an AIDS patient;
kissed an old person; visited the victim of a land-mine; and
we have been inspired by her compassion, as something we
recognize should be part of us all. Certainly, this cathedral and
every church in the diocese ought clearly to be a centre of such
compassion, and a centre of a variety of gifts.

'Enthusiasm is the gateway to adoration.' I heard Bishop
Ian Ramsey say that on one occasion. And adoration can be
the gateway to worship. The admiration of the gifts of the
Princess of Wales, the enthusiasm for her, is at least the gateway to worship, not of the Princess herself, but of the Giver of
all gifts, and of the One who can gather up the fragments of
our broken lives so that nothing be lost.

Last Sunday morning I was preaching – as I've said – at St
Saviour's, Pimlico. By chance, it was in the church hall of St
Saviour's that Princess Diana had taught in the kindergarten
there of a week-day, before her marriage. It was after the
service that a young man of about twenty came into the
church, bearing a bouquet of flowers and a message he had
written. 'Where could I put these?' he asked shyly. He told me

he was one of the children whom the Princess had looked after when he was a toddler. He had never forgotten her. He said: 'You know, there'll always be a place for her in my heart.' That was my first experience of the response which has now become an avalanche. It's a wonderful thing, surely, when someone can make such a mark of care on others.

'Every good gift and every perfect gift is from above,' wrote St James, 'and cometh down from the Father.'

But, alas, it won't do for us to stop there. This week's tragedy has some tough messages for us at the heart of it. And my sixth point must be the undeniable element of evil in the tragedy: the insatiable greed of the media, the cash involved in the desperate attempt to get photographs that will satisfy our demands – the public's demands, the market's demands. That, too, is part of the need for us to say 'Lord, have mercy' and to repent – not only in church but in action. It's a complex prayer, because so much of our world is curse and blessing: blessing and curse. The blessing of the media we saw only yesterday, in that remarkable televised service; the curse we saw a week earlier.

The 'ikon' – as it has so often been called this week – of Princess Diana could be dangerously unreal and romantic. The tragedy has not only been the death of the Princess. It has been the broken marriage, and, thereafter, understandably, the desperate, compulsive search for another companion and partner so that now two sons are motherless. The ikon, to be real, must be not only one of compassion for the poor, it must portray a crucifixion in a Mercedes, after a journey at, literally, break-neck speed, along a Via Dolorosa from the Ritz Hotel.

That, too, says something to a church which somehow has to be brave enough always to warn, but which must earn a name not primarily for judgment, but for understanding and mercy: a name which is not the church's name by right but the Name of Jesus, the ikon of God himself, the Compassionate God – who 'as His majesty is, so is His mercy'.

This cathedral, each church in the diocese, needs to be a

notable centre of reconciliation: where each person – each couple and partnership in need – know they will find skilled help and understanding when their relationships are strained to breaking point and beyond. (Not every cathedral is a notable centre of reconciliation!)

Seventhly: one of the constant themes of this week has been the clash between the private and the public worlds. How difficult it is to manage the contrast and conflict between them. If you are an MP, or a judge, or a royal, or indeed – as I know well – as a priest, the public/private connection is undeniably a problem. 'Don't photograph me, the private me. Let me have space for my private world.' Most of us have at least two selves, the private and the public. People say so often: 'What you do in private is your own affair.' But is it? Integrity is when there's no gap between the two worlds, and when we're not ashamed to have our private self exposed to the public gaze. Jesus had a private self, but it was manifest in his public self. He needed time to withdraw and be private, as we all do. A world that does not allow us to be private is cruel: criminally cruel.

The church must surely be a body in which we can learn about withdrawing, with intent to return to the world. Each church is a place of transfiguration: a place where space and silence must be given to all who need it, a place where our integrity and integration is continually deepened. And Christians have a precious truth to teach: you are never alone in the presence of God.

And now to my last point, the last item on my shopping list. We live not only in the two worlds of the private and the public. We live in the world of time into which eternity breaks through. And time is the raw material of eternity.

Time: The Princess – our vulnerable Princess – was, alas, only thirty-six years old.

Time: A week – such as we have just passed through – is a long time.

Time: It takes time to come to terms with an event like the death of Princess Diana – not just one week. The young princes will take a long time to come to terms with their mother's death. Perhaps they never will. But so, too, will Prince Charles, and all the Royal Family.

Time: Shakespeare – Southwark's Shakespeare – said, in a Sonnet:

> Time will come and take my love away.
> This thought is as a death
> Which cannot choose but weep to have
> That which it fears to lose.

Time: We are gathered here, today, and, now, in time, and in this place, because here in particular we are in touch with Eternity: that is, in part, what prayer and worship is.

We heard yesterday in that memorable service, in one of the poems: 'For those who love, Time is Eternity'. That was the sentence I took away from the service.

We give thanks today for this cathedral church – which, like so many others – has been a gateway to eternity – for hundreds; for thousands – all these years.

We give thanks today for the patron saint of this Church of St Saviour with St Mary Overie, Mary, the Mother of our Lord, who, in her Son's hour of need stood by him: stood by his cross. She, surely, will understand what Princess Diana has gone through, and Prince Charles, and the two boys, and all the Royal Family – and us all.

Look at the memorials on these walls – from John Gower to Sam Wannamaker. They are all memorials of Time, but they are of people now in the keeping of him who is eternal love: Love like the love the crucified Jesus displayed.

After such a week as this, we all need, surely, to commend and commit ourselves afresh to him who is eternal love: our creator and redeemer, the author and perfecter – the finisher – of our life. Our beginning and our end – our end: Princess Diana's end. In the end, God is her hope and the hope of us all.

35

'A Door was Opened in Heaven'

Farlington Parish Church, Portsmouth;
26 October 1997

'A door was opened in heaven.'
Revelation 4.1

I wonder if you were asked to say if any experience has ever opened a door in heaven for you, what your answer would be? To be honest, I'd like to spend a whole weekend with you, listening to your answers to that question. It's a question I've asked different people from time to time. Some people simply look blank. Others answer immediately and certainly. Others begin hesitantly to put into words some experience which it's clearly not easy for them to articulate.

On Wednesday evening this last week, I went to see the new-born baby of two people – Alice and Mark – whom I'd married last year. Alice had just come out of hospital. As I held their baby in my arms, it seemed to me a small miracle. The father of the baby is an oil engineer out in Nigeria. He's Dutch, and has had a mainly scientific upbringing and education. I think that being a father – the father of that child – has already introduced him to new dimensions. I don't think he'd say 'A door has opened in heaven' – those are not his sort of words; but he'd say he's having to think about what human life is in quite a new way: the human life that would not exist without him and Alice.

I've baptized two other children in that family, two children of Alice's sister, Gina. But Gina's first baby I had to baptize in a hospital ward in West London. She was severely brain damaged at birth – and, of course, still is. She'll never be able to talk. Looking after her now demands a very great deal, and she's much loved. But . . . But . . . the future is very uncertain.

In this world, it's not long before you meet with suffering, and your prayer to God is often a heartfelt cry. Much like Jesus' cry on the cross, it's often simply an agonizing question: 'Why?' But sometimes that agony, that agonizing situation, seems to 'open a door in heaven' that a more placid and prosperous life has never done, and, probably, would never do. Gina and Hugo's way of life has been utterly altered by the birth of their child.

When I ask that question: 'What has opened a door in heaven for you?' there are widely differing answers. Some will cite, say, a particular piece of music on a particular occasion. Some will relate how, out walking in the country, the world one day seemed suddenly to be unreal, and they were overtaken by a feeling of being out of time, and literally in heaven, for perhaps only a matter of seconds.

Sometimes it's a good experience which has seemed as though it has opened a door in heaven. Sometimes it's because the world – and life around – seemed so bad and out of joint, that heaven has suddenly become real. Sometimes, when you come to talk to people about what prayer means for them, they cite a particular experience: an extraordinary experience.

The text: 'A door was opened in heaven' comes from the last book of the Bible, from, as we've said, the Book of the Revelation of St John the Divine. It's not an easy book to understand. The best commentary on it I know was written by a German bishop, Hans Lilje, one of the most courageous opponents of Naziism. He wrote most of his commentary in prison, whilst he was in the hands of the Gestapo. He found, not unnaturally, that what St John the Divine had written, probably in exile, on the tiny island of Patmos – an island about ten miles long and six miles wide – spoke to his condition and to his situation.

It's worth noting that John the Divine had his experience of a 'door opening in heaven' on what I will call an ordinary Sunday morning, like this. It became a memorable Sunday morning, a unique Sunday in the whole history of the church of God; but John wasn't expecting it to be a different Sunday. It was a Sunday like today. But then, without warning, John had a vision: of the Lord of the whole universe and of history, seated in majesty upon his throne, in radiance and glory. John claimed he saw the Lord through, as it were, an open door. Of course, vision and reality are not the same. But what John saw then meant for him that there was no doubt at all who's in charge of the universe.

Bishop Hans Lilje tells how when he wrote his commentary on the Book of the Revelation it became ludicrous to him to imagine that Hitler was the ultimate authority in this world, any more than for John the Divine the Roman empire was the last word. Who was in charge became blindingly clear to him.

Sometimes we are given spiritual gifts just when we most need them; and they encourage us, and strengthen our faith. That's what happened to John the Divine and to Bishop Hans Lilje: and through them we can be encouraged.

On this Sunday in the church's year, we're doing what the Old Testament as well as the New teaches us to do. The writers of the Old Testament reflected on the course of history from its very beginning. They knew that the world is not purposeless, is not without a cause. They knew that the world has a Creator, and therefore that it has a Lord; and because they worshipped this Creator and Lord they began to recognize his activity in their world and in their own lives, no matter what the top surface of events at first looked like. At first sight, John on the Isle of Patmos might have had a very different view of life – a very depressing one; but as he began to worship the Lord of Creation on the Lord's day his eyes were opened. A door was opened – as he worshipped.

We don't know precisely what form the worship took that Sunday where John was. It would not be surprising if he had been using, for instance, the Psalms which bear witness to God's wonders of creation in this world. John's faith, although it was in the Lord of Creation and the Lord of history, would certainly not have been a faith in God to be worked out only in this life, in this world. This world is so often the scene of death and destruction, indeed, of unmitigated evil.

John looked – and lo, in heaven an open door. And the first voice which he heard speaking to him was like a trumpet which said: Come up hither and I will show you what must take place after this: after this world, not simply in this world now.

People's faith, in our generation, has become to my mind too this-worldly. We're not just thankful for this world, we're besotted by it. Now life in this world is very important. What we do about this world we live in is very important. But it's only part of the whole, part of all the universe that God has in his hands.

On Thursday evening this last week I went to the Old Vic, to see again my favourite play, Shakespeare's *King Lear*. Whenever I see it, I wait to hear the marvellous instruction that Shakespeare gives us. He says we're to

> take upon's the mystery of things,
> As if we were God's spies.

That's exactly what John the Divine did. 'After this, I looked, and, behold, a door was opened in heaven.'

As human beings we have to have our eyes open to the mystery of things as if we were God's spies. The mystery of this world which opens up on to an even larger world than this. Whatever your main subject at school, or university, whatever your job is, wherever your home is, whatever your circumstances are, all of us have to take upon us the mystery of things as if we were God's spies. To be truly human is to say more and more profoundly, 'I spy with my little eye'.

And a door will be opened for us in heaven: maybe as it was for John on just such a Sunday as this, in just such a church as this. Maybe this door will be opened for us through what seems an entirely secular experience, an entirely this-worldly experience.

But remember always: we're not just churchgoers, we're God's spies, always. And spies of all sorts need, of course, a great deal of training, otherwise we may never see the door opened in heaven. We may 'miss the many splendoured thing' that God has prepared for us. John the Divine said for him one ordinary Sunday like this: 'A door was opened in heaven.'

36

Bishop Walsham How

Westminster Abbey; 2 November 1997

I've been preaching about the saints for nearly fifty years now, and I've never found it easy. I'm aware that most people think of saints as miles away from themselves, or think of themselves as miles away from being a saint. And my task is particularly difficult this year, because I want to preach to you about a Victorian bishop, who I think knew a thing or two about sanctity; but as this year is the centenary of his death, I specially want to commemorate him: not least because he wrote the great hymn 'For all the saints who from their labours rest'.

William Walsham How, later Bishop How, was born in 1823, in Shrewsbury, that lovely town on the banks of the river Severn. His mother died when he was only two and a half.

Walsham How began his hymn-writing early, before he was thirteen. He was a keen young gardener and botanist, drying and mounting species of wild flowers, and he founded a horticultural society at Shrewsbury School. So it's not surprising that the first hymn he ever wrote is of the transformation of the butterfly from a chrysalis, as a parable of the resurrection.

While still at school, having matriculated to Oxford, he was a candidate for the Newdigate Prize Poem. At Oxford, he holidayed in Ireland with a fellow undergraduate, the tormented young poet Arthur Hugh Clough. After Oxford, Walsham How read Divinity at Durham, where he met his future wife, Frances, the eldest daughter of a canon of

Durham. In 1848 he was ordained to a curacy at Kidder-
minster, where Thomas Legh Claughton was vicar and then,
later, Bishop of Rochester and then of St Albans. Within two
years, Walsham How returned to Shrewsbury for a second
curacy, where he married Frances Douglas, and where the first
volume of his *Plain Words* was published, which were to
make him known as an author throughout the land.

In 1851 he was instituted to the country living of Whittington, outside Oswestry, where he was to stay for twenty-eight
years.

During a family holiday, at Barmouth, one of his two sons,
only three years old, died, and was buried there.

Although Walsham How was for most of his ministry a
country parson, and, literally, a rural dean, his work was not
confined to his parish. He was elected to Convocation in 1868,
the year after he had been offered the bishopric of Natal in
South Africa. In 1873 the Archbishop of Canterbury pressed
him to become Bishop of Cape Town. He was also asked to be
the vicar of All Saints', Margaret Street. He had declined the
bishopric of Montreal in 1879, when he was fifty-five, instead
being appointed suffragan bishop of the whole of the East End
of London – which we now know as 'Stepney', but was then
styled, quite ridiculously, for legal reasons, as Bedford.

It has to be said that Mrs Walsham How suffered dreadfully from asthma and bronchitis, and it may well have been
that which kept her husband at Whittington, though 'kept' is
a slight exaggeration. He did long chaplaincies at Rome and at
Cannes, in France, 'wintering' there sometimes, to use his own
word; and he became a notable conductor of retreats and a
leader of missions throughout the land. He became not only a
hymn-writer – and many of his hymns were clearly written for
his Missions – but in the early 1870s he became a hymn book
editor. He edited *Church Hymns*, one of the main hymn books
of the day, published by the SPCK.

In the *Church Hymnary* of 1898, Walsham How had sixteen hymns, of which I find in my own life-time I have learnt,
and learnt to love, at least six:

'For all the saints'; 'Soldiers of the Cross arise'; 'Summer suns are glowing' (which I particularly loved as a child). And those that I suggest had their origin as mission hymns: 'O my Saviour lifted from the earth for me'; 'It is a thing most wonderful'; and 'O Jesus, thou art standing outside the fast-closed door', which clearly owes the details of the picture it paints to Holman Hunt's famous painting 'The Light of the World' painted in 1854, now in St Paul's Cathedral and Keble College, Oxford.

Of course, hymns owe their popularity as much to their tunes as to their words. 'For all the saints' began with a tune by Sir Joseph Barnby, was refreshed by one composed by Stanford, but reached its zenith by way of Ralph Vaughan Williams' great tune composed for the *English Hymnal* in 1906, which has surely extended the life of the hymn by at least a century.

I think that if our life is centred on Walsham How's hymn 'It is a thing most wonderful', there's quite a possibility that we may be numbered amongst 'all the saints who' he says' 'from their labours rest':

It is a thing most wonderful,
    Almost too wonderful to be,
That God's own Son should come from heaven,
    And die to save a child like me.

And yet I know that it is true:
    He chose a poor and humble lot,
And wept, and toiled, and mourned, and died
    For love of those who loved him not.

But even could I see him die,
    I could but see a little part
Of that great love, which, like a fire,
    Is always burning in his heart.

> It is most wonderful to know
>   His love for me so free and sure;
> But 'tis more wonderful to see
>   My love for him so faint and poor.
>
> And yet I want to love thee, Lord;
>   O light the flame within my heart,
> And I will love thee more and more,
>   Until I see thee as thou art.

Yes: if that hymn becomes part of you, I think you're on the way to sanctity.

The last period of Walsham How's life can be divided into two equal periods, each of nine years: the first, from his consecration as Bishop Suffragan of East London, in 1879; and the second, from his enthronement as the first Bishop of the new diocese of Wakefield, in 1888.

His title as Bishop of Bedford was, understandably, always a source of annoyance to him. Bedford was fifty miles north of London where his heavy responsiblities lay. His whole area of East London was, in those days, one of abject poverty and of congested population: an utterly different world from his first twenty-eight years of ministry.

Walsham How thought of his job as the leader of an East London Crusade. He immediately set up the East London Church Fund, which was launched at the Mansion House in 1880. It began to supply curates to large parishes; it saw to the division of large parishes and the supply of mission clergy; it enabled the aged clergy to retire, and provided for lay workers, male and female. The Bishop made it clear that the East London Church Fund needed the support of the wealthy areas of the diocese, and, indeed, of the wealthy areas of other dioceses. He preached in places like Brighton and Bournemouth on behalf of East London.

His new home was in Upper Clapton, and he and his wife kept open house for the clergy every Thursday. He soon got a name for visiting the clergy in their own homes, and was called the 'omnibus' bishop for going everwhere he could by that means of transport.

Besides being Bishop, he was incumbent of the Church of St Andrew Undershaft, in the City, which was how his episcopal stipend was provided. He became a member of the Royal Commission on the Housing of the Poor. He was a great supporter of the University Settlement in Stepney, Toynbee Hall, and of the university and college missions in East London.

In 1885 he was offered – but refused – the bishopric of Manchester. However, in the same year a new Bishop of London, Frederick Temple, was appointed, who clearly did not like the fact that, in effect, East London had been handed over to his suffragan bishop. In 1887 Walsham How's wife died, and when, in 1888, he was offered the new diocese of Wakefield, which had been carved out of the diocese of Ripon, although he had intended to stay in East London for the rest of his days, he decided to accept the offer. One thing is certain: no Bishop of the East End of London was ever more loved than Walsham How.

Wakefield, in Yorkshire, might be thought to be very different from East London – and is; but it was also remarkably similar. It was the centre of an industrialized and mining area, with a huge population. In 1893 there was a tragic pit disaster, and the Bishop shared in conducting the ninety-two funerals, in the parish of Thornhill, of the 137 miners who had been killed. He did all he could to bring to an end the great colliery strike that year.

Less than two years after going to Wakefield, in 1890, he was offered the bishopric of Durham, but was absolutely sure he would have been wrong to accept it, and refused it by return of post. He became as close to the clergy and people of Wakefield diocese as he had been to those of East London.

It was on Easter Eve, 1897, the year of Queen Victoria's Diamond Jubilee, that he received a letter from the Prince of Wales at Sandringham:

April 16 1897

Dear Bishop of Wakefield,

It is proposed that a special hymn should be composed to be sung in all our churches, both at home and abroad, on June 20, the day on which the Queen attains the sixtieth year of her reign. I write these lines to ask you whether you will kindly consent to compose this hymn. Sir Arthur Sullivan has consented to compose the music, and is also most anxious that the hymn should be sent to all the colonies. Forgive my troubling you at such a busy time of the year for you, and, believe me,

Sincerely yours,
Albert Edward

The Bishop felt much honoured by the request, but was considerably alarmed at the difficulty of composing a hymn to order. When the hymn was published, he was nevertheless greatly amused when a typical Yorkshireman talked to him about it. 'It's a very difficult matter,' said the Bishop, 'to write a good hymn to order.' 'Impossible,' said the Yorkshireman – and said no more. A sense of humour and sanctity do not always go together.

Sullivan wrote the tune to the hymn and called it 'Bishop-garth', – the name of the Bishop's house in Wakefield.

Here's just a verse of the hymn:

> O King of Kings, whose reign of old
>   Hath been from everlasting;
> Before whose throne their crowns of gold
>   The white robed saints are casting;
> While all the shining courts on high
>   With angel songs are ringing
> Oh let thy children venture high
>   Their lowly homage bringing.

The Queen's Diamond Jubilee was celebrated on 23 June

1897. The Bishop was reluctant to face the exertion of the journey to London, and stayed in Wakefield to address his own people. That August, he went on holiday to Ireland, to County Mayo, with his family. Once there, he quickly grew weak, and died on 10 August 1897.

Why do I think Bishop Walsham How has something of the saint about him? Well, I think his commitment and devotion to that small parish is quite an example to be followed. I think his comitment to and readiness to serve areas of poverty is also an example to us. I've already suggested that his hymns show where his heart lay. That title the 'omnibus' bishop suggests a basic simplicity of life, and true simplicity always brings us close to sanctity. His Jubilee hymn suggests he had a sense of God as the Lord of all history, as the Lord of all creation, and as King of Kings. That's an attitude that was basic to all the prophets. It has animated many of the martyrs of our own time.

I am myself glad of this opportunity to celebrate with you the centenary of William Walsham How, who has rather been forgotten, even though people still sing his hymns. Let us this evening remember him as we sing now his hymn:

> For all the saints who from their labours rest,
> Who thee by faith before the world confest,
> Thy name, O Jesu, be for ever blest:
> Alleluya.

37

The Watch-tower

Westminster Abbey; 9 November 1997

'I will climb my watch-tower.'
Habakkuk 2.1

Nothing is known about the prophet Habakkuk except his approximate date. The allusion to the Chaldeans in various verses of its three chapters places the book within a few years of 600 BC. But it's a notable book, because it begins with a dialogue in which the prophet has the courage seriously to question God's justice. He wants to know how can God allow the wicked Chaldeans to triumph. Later in the book he utters a series of denunciations of human injustice which begin with 'Woe'. But the verse which began our reading this evening is a wonderful word-picture of religion at its best: 'I will climb my watch-tower and wait to see what the Lord will tell me to say and what answer he will give to my complaint.'

We no longer live in a world in which watch-towers are things we talk of every day, though under new names they form as important a part of our life, at, say, Heathrow, as they ever did. A lot of the work of the look-out has, of course, been taken over by technology. But I want to suggest that that first verse depicts and describes one of the inalienable tasks, capacities, responsibilities of being human. 'I will climb my watch-tower and wait to see what the Lord will tell me to say and what answer he will give to my complaint.' It's a marvellous verse not least because it combines action and contemplation.

It was an Irishman, a Dubliner, who said in 1790: 'The condition upon which God hath given liberty to man is eternal vigilance.' 'I will climb my watch-tower' suggests effort, strenuous effort, maybe grim effort, resolution, relentless effort, choice, discipline, vigilance: the prophet is clearly no layabout. He has decided to bestir himself.

He will go to the place of vision. And there is a suggestion that he has to 'rise above' his usual world to do this: he has to ascend and transcend his usual self.

Of course: the watch-tower is a metaphor. But watching is one of the basic human activities and capacities which are both outward and visible and inward and spiritual and mental. Watching means seeing instead of being blind: contemplating, observing, instead of being insensitive to this and that; and it's at the heart of being human.

Karl Marx said: 'Only a participant is a profound observer'. But that needs to be complemented by 'The man on the touch-line sees most of the game.' Climbing the watch-tower has a suggestion of going to the touch line.

The watch-tower has also the suggestion of the awareness of danger to it. It's a look-out. And 'Look Out!' often has the suggestion of danger to it. There's expectation to it – not necessarily of good. Watch – look – 'I looked the other way' – see – seer – visionary – 'Whereas I was blind, now I see.'

St Augustine said: 'We shall see and we shall love.' But that was talking of the vision of God. In this world, sometimes we shall see and we shall loathe, or we shall see and be terrified. 'Look! – Do you see what I see?' It was an artist who said: 'You must look and look until your eyes bleed.'

When you're on duty on the watch-tower, there may be many who depend on you, depend on your watching. So I say again: that first verse speaks to me of someone who has discovered what he has to do as a human being in this world. 'I will climb my watch-tower . . .' Sometimes it helps to do something like that in company, with friends. 'Next weekend let's go to, say, the Bird Sanctuary and do some watching together.'

But I think there's an inescapable loneliness – or, at least, alone-ness, being alone – for the prophet in each one of us. 'I will climb my watch-tower, come what may' . . . 'And wait to see what the Lord will tell me to say.'

Waiting on God was the title of a great book by Simone Weil. Born in Paris, she died, aged only forty, in 1943. She taught philosophy, but interspersed this with periods of hard manual labour on farms and at the Renault works, in order to experience working-class life. In 1936 she served in the Republican forces in the Spanish Civil War. In 1941 she settled in Marseilles, where she befriended the Dominican priest Henri Perrin. She had a deep mystical feeling for the Catholic faith, coupled with a profound reluctance to join any organized religion. She was never baptized. She escaped to England in 1942 and worked for the Free French in London before her death, in Kent, in 1943. I think immediately of such a person when I think of Habakkuk: – 'I will climb my watch-tower and wait to see what the Lord will tell me to say and what answer he will give to my complaint.'

I only got one prize when I was at university – at King's College, London – but I'm very proud of it, because it's a book I've treasured for nearly fifty years. It's called *The Truth of Vision: A Study in the Nature of Christian Hope.* It's by Max Warren, who was a Canon of Westminster after he'd been head of the Church Missionary Society. He was a profound thinker about not only church and state, but about Christians in various societies in the world today and various cultures. He died in 1977.

The Truth of Vision was published in 1948, and this is how it begins:

Habakkuk, like the other prophets of Israel, grappled with the perplexities and fears of his age. As he sought to find a meaning in contemporary events, God spoke to him and revealed Himself as the Lord of all history. From this revelation springs the Biblical understanding of Hope.

The application of this truth to our own age demands an attempt to achieve a sympathetic understanding of the events of our time and to see the Church set in the midst of those events to serve the purposes of God. This is no easy task. It is costly in sympathy and in patience.

The first result of such a sympathetic approach to events is that the Church is confronted by the fact of secular hopefulness and is forced to discover a fresh understanding of the nature of its own hope.

In fact, there's a danger in thinking of Habakkuk as one of the great prophets of Israel, and thinking of this text as part of the thought of a great prophet.

I've half suggested already that I think we need to see ourselves in this verse. In the last few weeks there have been several personal situations in which I've felt there's only one thing to do: to climb my watch-tower and wait to see what the Lord would tell me to say.

I have climbed my watch-tower to see what the Lord will tell me to say and what answer he will give to my complaint.

Now let me tell you about D. and B., – who've been on my mind this week. Husband and wife, both well into their eighties. And they have both been marvellous servants of the church of God. During the war they both helped with a club for down-and-outs under Hungerford Bridge. B., the husband, was, as it happens, Canon Max Warren's right-hand man at the Church Missionary Society, serving him with love and diligence. D., his wife, was churchwarden at St Mary's, Lambeth, close to Lambeth Palace, for many years, and both of them steered St Mary's as it was closed down, to become a joint church with the Methodists down the road – a hugely difficult undertaking, people being people.

But D. was also chair of one of the major local Lambeth historical charities. For several years it was clear she had Alzheimer's Disease, and for all this year she has been in care, with B. visiting her every day, several miles there and several miles back. She was moved from a home in Clapham a few days ago to another in Newcastle-upon-Tyne to be nearer their daughter. B. moves to Newcastle in a few days to be nearer his wife and family. Though it could be worse, it's surely a cruel ending of the day for two aged people.

I have climbed my watch-tower to see what the Lord will say to me and what answer he will give to my complaint.

Some events more than others cause you to climb your watch-tower – not to escape but in search of a wisdom wiser than your own. And, maybe, to see 'what answer God will give to your complaint'. Sometimes it's a personal event. Sometimes it's a social event, that's to say, something that affects several or many persons, maybe multitudes. Not only in war time but in peace time we need to climb our watch-towers.

In the case of Habakkuk it was the Chaldeans who caused him to climb his watch-tower: to retreat to it. Retreat is not always a negative word in the Christian vocabulary.

You can go on retreat – say, once a year. You can climb your watch-tower for a considerable length of time. Or you can make it part of your regular daily or weekly regime and discipline. As a priest, I feel it an obligation to climb my watch-tower. But a priest is really a representative person. I personify something which is true of all, and my job is to encourage and assist everyone to discover their priesthood in their humanity: to discover how they, that's to say you, with your time-table and obligations, can best climb your watch-tower to see what the Lord will tell you to say and what answer he will give to your complaint.

From your watch-tower you will get a different perspective and new dimensions.

In the Oxford Study Bible, the comment on this verse from Habakkuk is: 'The prophet sees himself as the outpost of human consciousness to pick up God's faintest message to humanity and regards himself as a responsible spokesman for humanity before God.' That says a lot about prayer as well as about prophecy; about prayer and humanity; about being truly human.

One of the best things I ever did was, thirty years ago, to ask Alan Ecclestone, then a priest in the diocese of Sheffield, to give a talk on prayer. It was the best I'd ever heard, the most helpful to me. He died in 1992. I want to end what I have to say by quoting a paragraph from that talk.

> Prayer is a kind of observing. It is part of our Christian calling to
>
> > take upon's the mystery of things,
> > As if we were God's spies
>
> and to develop the kind of seeing without which we cannot be said to be responsive to God at all. In the practice of prayer focussed upon the stuff of everyday experience, we may learn to see particularly and distinctly the nature of things, discriminating and appraising in an ever more and more sensitive fashion. When Peguy in one of his poems put into the mouth of God the observation, 'If there were no Frenchmen, some things I do would never be seen,' he was thus indicating the extreme importance for spiritual growth of this learning to see.

If there were no one with your name and personality some things that God wants to happen in his world would not happen. But we need to be in touch with God to make as sure as we can that what happens is what he wants to happen.

'I will climb my watch-tower and wait to see what the Lord will tell me to say and what answer he will give to my complaint.'

38

Bishop George Bell and the Kingdom of Christ

Christ the Kings, Haldens, Welwyn Garden City;
The Feast of Christ the King, 23 November 1997

The hymn 'Christ is the King! O friends rejoice' – which we shall be singing later – might have been specially written for your Patronal Festival today. Actually, it was written for the hymn book *Songs of Praise* in 1926 – and, later, revised into its present form. And the man who wrote the hymn – George Kennedy Allen Bell, Bishop of Chichester from 1929 to 1958 – has, I believe, a special message for us at your Festival. In fact, in 1954, George Bell wrote a book called *The Kingship of Christ,* and, in the First World War, edited a book called *The War and the Kingdom of Christ;* so your theme of Christ the King – which gives its name to your church – was very much his.

In the First World War book, Bell wrote that it isn't enough to put all your energies into the war, because you're sure that England's on the side of law, justice and liberty. The cause of the Kingdom of God is greater even than the cause of the patriot. It's the one reign and rule which is able to put an end to the misery and tyranny of war. It calls us all to repentance of the sins from which war springs, and it points to a hope beyond our national and international struggles.

George Bell was the son of a parson. After school and university he was ordained to a curacy at Leeds Parish Church, which in those days gave him a serious concern for the social problems of the day. After Leeds, Bell went back to Oxford, to do a pastoral job amongst students for a few years, and then he became chaplain to the Archbishop of Canterbury, Randall Davidson – on the eve of the outbreak of the First World War, in 1914.

In Bell's ten years at Lambeth, he grew into one of the great Christian leaders of our time. His two brothers, and many of his Oxford pupils and friends, were killed in the war, and there's no doubt that those terrible losses gave Bell a mission for life: the mission of the Kingdom of Christ.

At Lambeth, Bell began the great work of his life with the other Christian leaders of the nation. He got to know most of the secular leaders of society, not least the Prime Ministers of the day. He helped to draft, with the great social historian, R. H. Tawney, the report *Christianity and Industrial Problems*. He was so superb at his job at Lambeth that many of the eminent men of his day, in church and state, felt that he ought to be a bishop straight away – or even archbishop – when he had done his ten years at Lambeth. But, instead, he was made Dean of Canterbury. While at Lambeth, in 1917, Bell fell in love with someone who worked at Lambeth, Henrietta Livingstone – known to all as Hettie. They married in January 1918, and Hettie was a wonderful wife to George.

Already Bell had probably done more than anyone in Britain to help the churches to unite. He worked very hard at the movement which resulted in the World Council of Churches, with people like the great Swedish Archbishop of Uppsala, Nathan Söderblom. It was unthinkable to Bell that anyone really concerned with the Kingdom of Christ should be satisfied with a divided church.

As Dean of Canterbury, Bell was able to continue that work; and his work concerned not just church unity but world unity and order in those crucial post-war years.

But one of Bell's greatest concerns at Canterbury was with quite another aspect of the Kingdom of Christ: poetry, drama, music, and the arts. T. S. Eliot's great verse play *Murder in the Cathedral* about the martyrdom of Thomas à Becket at Canterbury; John Masefield's play *The Coming of Christ*;

Dorothy L. Sayers' *The Zeal of Thine House,* were all produced at Canterbury through the initiative of the Dean.

Bell's five creative years at Canterbury were followed by
twenty-eight years as Bishop of Chichester. He was a much-
loved pastor there; but he was not only a diocesan bishop, he
was now a national and international leader, come to his full
stature and maturity.

In the 1930s, he tried to give all the support he could to that
part of the church in Germany – the 'Confessing' Church, as it
was called – that was confronting and resisting Hitler. That
led him to an unremitting commitment to the victims of Nazi
persecution – to the Jews, but also to other victims who came
as refugees to this country, not least to the many Christian
priests and pastors who would otherwise have ended their
lives in Nazi concentration camps.

I can never myself forget how, as a teenager, I would regularly go round to our local vicarage, where lived one such
pastor, Heinz Helmut Arnold. He had come to us in 1938, his
hands raw with the results of frost-bite from working in a
quarry just outside the concentration camp where he was
imprisoned. He would often speak of the courage of his friend
Pastor Niemöller of Dahlem, Berlin; but he would also speak
of what the friendship and support of George Bell had meant
to him: getting him to England, and looking after him here.

One German pastor in particular George Bell befriended –
Dietrich Bonhoeffer, who in 1933 was for a year the minister
to the German congregation in London, at their church at
Forest Hill. During the Second World War, in 1942, Bell
secretly met with Bonhoeffer in Sweden. At that meeting,
Bonhoeffer passed to Bell the details of the conspiracy of
German officers against Hitler – which Bell passed to the
British Government. By then, however, the Allies were
only interested in 'unconditional surrender'. Eventually,
Bonhoeffer was executed, on 9 April 1945, in a concentration
camp, sending a last message, just before his death, to George
Bell.

During the Second World War, Bell showed his courage not

only by that journey to Sweden. He made speeches in the House of Lords which made him – like his Lord – 'of no reputation'.

Bell spoke out against indiscriminate bombing and a spirit of vengeance. His speeches aroused strong feelings, even in his own diocese. Bell was due to preach one year on Battle of Britain Sunday in his own cathedral, but the Dean asked him not to preach. It was those speeches during the war that destroyed Bell's chance of succeeding William Temple as Archbishop of Canterbury when Temple suddenly died, in 1944. There's little doubt that it was Churchill's personal opposition to Bell that prevented his following Temple as Archbishop; but there are few now who think that decision was just or right.

Bell became such an important bishop on the national and international scene that it's easy to forget now that for twenty-eight years he served Christ the King in the day-to-day work of a diocesan bishop.

Some of you may perhaps know that I was close to Bishop John Robinson. It interested me that Bell – as Dean of Canterbury – conducted John Robinson's father's funeral when John was a boy of eleven. His father had been a Canon of Canterbury when Bell was Dean. In 1945, when the young John Robinson was perplexed as to whether he should go to a parish as his first job after ordination or go to an academic job, he sought the advice of Bishop Bell. After giving him unhurried time, and clear advice to go first to a parish and earth his academic theology in experience in the world, Bell said to him, late at night: 'Now let me read you some poetry'!

It was in 1954, four years before he died, that George Bell wrote, in less than twelve weeks, his book *The Kingship of Christ*, which was published as a Penguin 'Special' at two shillings. It sold 36,000 copies. I doubt whether I could do better to end what I have to say to you at your Festival of Christ the King than by reading some sentences from the very end of what George Bell has to say in that book. Most of the book is about the Kingdom of Christ in this world; but, not long before he died, Bell is writing, at the end of his book, about the world beyond this one. He says:

> The character of the new age cannot be expressed in the language of ordinary prose. But the believer is quite sure that God's promises will be fulfilled, that the purpose of God revealed in Christ crucified will be seen, with a clarity that even the blindest cannot miss, as everywhere triumphant; and that 'the new life" in Christ will be fulfilled at the end of history.
>
> The New Testament uses the language of symbols, images and pictures in describing this fulfilment; and the images used by New Testament writers have been all too often developed in fantastic ways . . . But the truth is greater than the form in which it is presented; and the truth is that the future lies with Jesus Christ . . .
>
> We do not know what are the limits of human achievement, of our own personal history, or of the history of the race. We do not know what possibilities are in store for us or what time is before us. We do know, however, that there is a limit, for we must all die. If we do not know Christ, death is the only limit we know. But with Christ death is transcended. He who has died for us and is alive for us, confronts us with a totally new reality, a new limit, a new boundary to our existence. With him and in him the new world has begun.

It's because he believed that, that George Bell could write his hymn: 'Christ is the King! O friends rejoice'. I might end there – and maybe I should! – but I'd prefer to end with another personal memory.

Hettie Bell gave all George Bell's episcopal robes and 'impedimenta' to Bishop John Robinson when he was consecrated Bishop of Woolwich. John was very proud of them. He proudly used George Bell's robe case wherever he went for the rest of his life. He stuck a bit of plaster over the words 'Bishop of Chichester' and wrote on the plaster 'Bishop of Woolwich'.

I'm wearing Bishop John Robinson's surplice this morning, and I think the stole I'm wearing was George Bell's. Anyhow, what I'm wearing makes me think thankfully and affectionately of John Robinson and George Bell and of 'those whom we love but see no longer' and makes me so glad to be with you all to preach to you, and to join in singing with you:

> Christ is the King! O friends rejoice;
> Brother and sisters, with one voice
> Make all men know he is your choice:
> > Alleluya

> Let love's unconquerable might
> God's people everywhere unite
> In service to the Lord of light:
> > Alleluya

39

Gerontius and Judgment

St Alban's, Holborn; First Sunday in Advent,
30 November 1997

Last Wednesday evening, part of me would have loved to have
been at St Paul's Cathedral for the performance of Elgar's *The
Dream of Gerontius;* but I had what they call 'a transcendent
obligation' to attend the induction of a friend as the incumbent of St Saviour's, Pimlico.

There were several reasons why I would have loved to have
been at St Paul's. I first heard *Gerontius* – that masterpiece
of Elgar's – on Saturday afternoon, 10 May 1941. The Royal
Choral Society was the choir. They had migrated during those
most dangerous months of the war from the Royal Albert
Hall to the Queen's Hall, next to Broadcasting House. I can
remember Dr Malcolm Sargent – as he was then – conducting.
The orchestra was the London Philharmonic. Webster Booth
was Gerontius. Muriel Brunskill, the Angel; and Ronald Stear,
the Priest and the Angel of the Agony. I was just sixteen.

I was taken to the performance by a great friend of mine,
John Rowe, a young ordinand, to whom I owe more than I can
say. He had left training for ordination with the Community
of the Resurrection at Mirfield, temporarily, to join up. He
was stationed at the Duke of York's Headquarters in Sloane
Square. In later years – before his untimely death in 1970,
when he was only fifty – John gained a double first in classics
at Leeds, and, after ordination and his curacy, became Vice-
Principal of Wells Theological College, then vicar of St
Mary's, Bathwick. But that unforgettable afternoon in 1941,
his birthday present to me was to take me to *Gerontius* as I've

said, for the first time. We parted quickly after the performance: he, to go on duty at Sloane Square; I, to get home, before
dark, to Chadwell Heath in Essex. Hardly was I home when
the siren went, and for five moonlit hours the German
bombers dropped a huge number of incendiaries and high
explosives on London. One thousand five hundred people
were killed that night, and rather more injured; and Queen's
Hall, the House of Commons, and many City Churches were
destroyed.

In October, 1947 – six years after that unforgettably terrible night – when I was still working at a riverside wharf on the
Thames, near Southwark Cathedral, and learning the organ
there, I heard *Gerontius* again, sung there by the Cathedral
Special Choir, with the young Kathleen Ferrier as the Angel.
Gerontius has remained for me, all the intervening years, not
only of great power for its music, but for its spiritual power
and quality.

It seems to me that Advent has many themes – certainly
four: Death, Judgment, Heaven and Hell – but it is important
that every one of us in Advent should confront again, and be
confronted by, the central message of Gerontius: an ordinary
person, at the point of death, facing judgment. His doubt
and fear, near to despair, meet with the unutterable Love of
God.

Elgar gave a copy of Newman's poem to his future wife, on
the occasion of her mother's death, in 1887. Newman himself
had written the poem, under the impact of the death in 1883
of a forty-one year-old friend, an Oratorian, Fr John Joseph
Gordon, who had said to Newman on his death-bed: 'I do not
say that I do not fear to die: for death must always be a fearful
thing. God's justice is very terrible; but then, in the crucifixion,
God's mercy appears so very great.'

I've never forgotten, from that first performance of
Gerontius in 1941, the very first phrase of Gerontius: 'Jesu,
Maria – I am near to death, And Thou art calling me.'

There's a certain sense in which we're always near to death
– all of us; life is very precarious, and Jesus and Mary are

always calling us. The call was very near that night of the 'blitz' in 1941; but 'near' is a very relative term.

On Elgar's own score of *Gerontius* he wrote some words of Virgil: 'Whence doth so dyre desire of Light on wretches grow?' And that lies at the heart of the whole theme of Judgment – our desire for that Light which is the Divine Love.

In the space of a single eucharistic sermon, I cannot draw your attention to all that *Gerontius* means to me. I want to suggest that as an Advent act of spiritual discipline you should try to listen to, say, someone's compact disc of *Gerontius*, and put yourself in the place of Gerontius. You'll have some demanding moments to go through. There's the demand on faith that enables Gerontius to sing, near the very beginning, the familiar words, which often trip off our tongue:

> Firmly I believe and truly
> God is Three, and God is One,
> And I next acknowledge duly
> Manhood taken by the Son.
> And I trust and hope most fully
> In that Manhood crucified . . .

And, at the end of that act of faith – there's the huge demand:

> And with a strong will I sever
> All the ties that bind me here.

As a priest, I have to say that those words of the priest at the end of the first part of Gerontius – 'Go forth upon thy journey, Christian soul' – always bring back to me many an occasion and many a person whom it's been my privilege to commend to God in their dying moments in this world, often with those words.

At the beginning of the second part of *Gerontius*, after his death, there's Newman's remarkable attempt to picture in words the world beyond time and space, as we know it. The soul of Gerontius is conscious that

> someone has me fast
> Within his ample palm. A uniform
> And gentle pressure tells me I am not
> Self-moving, but borne forward on my way . . .

And later, in answer to Gerontius' question:

> Shall I see
> My dearest Master, when I reach His Throne?

the Angel replies:

> Yes – for one moment thou shalt see thy Lord,
> One moment; but thou knowest not, my child,
> What thou dost ask: that sight of the Most Fair
> Will gladden thee, but it will pierce thee too.

Then, as the soul traverses the threshold, we hear the choir of Angels singing those other familiar words: 'Praise to the Holiest in the Height!'

I can rarely hear those words without thinking of the Radcliffe Hospital in Oxford, in March 1977. I was seeing out of this world John Clough, a dear friend, the twenty-four-year-old sub-organist at St Alban's Abbey, where I was then Canon Missioner. He was dying of leukaemia.

It was in the middle of that night that I started to recite various hymns which I knew John would have known and loved. I began to recite 'Praise to the Holiest . . .' When I got to 'O wisest Love' my memory suddenly failed. I said to the nurse with me in the ward: 'Can you remember how that hymn goes on?' 'No,' she replied. And we both felt we were meant to stop there with 'O wisest Love'. John died not long after we'd said those words.

After 'Praise to the Holiest' in *Gerontius* the Judgment is near; and then the Angel of the Agony prays for Gerontius – for us – that marvellous Litany:

Jesu! by that shuddering dread which fell on Thee . . .
Jesu! by that innocence which girdled Thee . . .
Jesu! by that sanctity that reigned in Thee . . .
Jesu! spare these souls which are so dear to Thee.

And then: the Judgment – which the soul himself beseeches, yet at which he cries 'Take me away . . .' And, gently, the Angel bears the soul of Gerontius away and takes care of him.

Judgment is always in the end what we ask for. It's always in the end a matter of the love of God: of the love of the living God. Judgment is always a matter of loving our Judge, and knowing that he can and will only be loving to us, for he is only – he is none other than, no less than – Love. It is all he is and all he has to give. So, let us ask this Advent, to understand God's loving judgment more profoundly. Ask to love your Judge more deeply.

The Angel says to Gerontius:

Learn that the flame of the Everlasting Love
Doth burn ere it transform.

People sometimes ask: 'Why *The Dream of Gerontius*? Was it a dream?' Well, the word 'dream' has, of course, several meanings. 'We are the music makers, and we are the dreamers of dreams,' says another work of Elgar's, *The Music Makers*. Dreams and dreamers there mean more a visionary than someone who gets ideas when he's asleep. *The Dream of Gerontius* to me is more the meditation of Gerontius; what came to him reflecting, maybe praying.

That's why I say to you: Listen this Advent to *Gerontius*, and as you do, pray not only for yourself but for 'those we love but see no longer' . . . John Henry Newman . . . Edward Elgar . . . Learn this Advent to love your Judge.

40

Baptism

St Giles, Camberwell; Third Sunday in Advent,
14 December 1997

The Gospel today is about baptism, about the crowds who came to be baptized by John the Baptist. What has baptism to say to us today?

Thinking about that question immediately makes me think of the baptism visits I used to do in your neighbouring parish of St George's, when I was its vicar nearly forty year ago. Several of those baptism visits still live in my memory.

There was the first baptism I ever took in St George's. The child was named Olayemi Olusola Odanye. I learnt the names off by heart, because I could never have pronounced them if I had not learnt them! And they've stuck in my memory all these years. Olayemi was Nigerian, and the family was living in just two rooms, in Boundary Lane, off the Walworth Road, literally on our parish boundary. The father was a medical student.

Not long ago, I gave a broadcast on the World Service of the BBC, and I spoke of that baptism. To my astonishment, within days, I had a letter from Olayemi, back in Nigeria, and another from his father. The son was now in his late thirties, the father nearly sixty. They were very delighted at the broadcast. Father said he'd never forgotten the baptism.

At the baptism I'd used a phrase of the Victorian theologian F. D. Maurice, who was a chaplain of Guy's Hospital and a Professor at King's College, London. He said: 'Baptism is the proclamation by God that this child is a child of mine.' I'd asked the congregation at St George's to do all they could to come to that baptism, because the neighbours of that Nigerian doctor – white people – had protested at the smell from his family's Nigerian cooking, which, they said, betokened the presence of the Devil! That baptism needed to proclaim, in the name of God, that 'this child is a child of mine'.

What else did we need to say in baptism? It interested me that, quite often, when I was doing baptism visits, the father, if he opened the door, would immediately say: 'Hang on: I'll get the wife.' I would quickly say: 'No. I want to talk to both of you.' But it would often be clear that it was the wife in particular who wanted the baby baptized. I used to wonder why that was. Are women more religious than men? I doubt it. But – maybe because the baby is, in a sense, more physically part of the mother and, even now, childbirth is still dangerous to baby and mother since something may still easily go wrong – perhaps that makes baptism a moment of thanksgiving and of awareness how precarious and fragile this life is, particularly to the mother.

The Christian church, it seems to me, provides a language and a liturgy, and an occasion to say 'Thank you' to Someone – with a capital 'S'. Babies often have baptism robes; but the whole of the baptism is a robe, a celebratory robe, for the unique event of this baby's birth. Yet at baptism fathers are often as full of delight as mothers.

When I came to St George's, Camberwell, there was a backlog of weddings to be taken. I remember interviewing David and his girl-friend about their wedding as soon as I arrived. It so happened that the Probation Officer came into the vicarage just as David and his girl went out. 'Why have you been seeing him so soon?' the Probation Officer asked me. I told him: I'd been preparing them for marriage. He told me that David was well known locally as a member of a violent gang. I said: 'Well, he's been very docile today!'

It wasn't all that long after David's wedding that one day, as I made my way from the vicarage to the bus stop, through Addington Square, David opened a window and called out to me: 'Vicar! Come up and see the baby!' We stood by the cot while David kept on saying how marvellous it was. A few weeks later we baptized the baby.

I think that being loved by his girl-friend, now his wife, and having a baby to look after, had completely changed David's life. It had taught David who he is as no other lesson could. When he said the baby was 'marvellous', he meant it. He'd learnt at first hand the meaning of wonder. But he'd learnt something about himself as well. Baptism wasn't a narrowly religious commitment: it was for David a public promise to be committed to the upbringing and welfare of that baby and that family.

One of the characters in one of Shakespeare's plays simply says: 'Thy life's a miracle.' Baptism is a way of saying that about a child; but as we say it, it reminds us that our life, too, is a miracle.

I know that one of your congregation here, now very old, is Cecilia Goodenough. When I was a vicar at St George's, she lived in our parish and worked at a huge hostel for the homeless, on the borders of the parish, called Newington Lodge – a ghastly Dickensian place. Thinking of Cecilia reminds me of another baptism.

A woman called at the vicarage one day and said, standing at the door, holding her baby: 'Could you christen my baby?' I said: 'Yes – but I shall need to know where you live.' 'Newington Lodge,' she replied. I was not surprised when she told me her husband had left her; but when we talked about god-parents she came out with the searingly unforgettable phrase: 'I haven't got any friends.'

What was clear was that she was used to being rejected. She was a 'bird of passage', and the likelihood of the baby receiving a stable Christian upbringing was small. But that baptism enabled us, as a congregation, to do two things. First: to get some of the congregation to think of, and try to treat that woman and her child as theirs to care for and love, in Christ's name. Baptism proclaimed that we all belonged to one another – we were 'members one of another'. Secondly: we were able to proclaim to that woman that her homeless, fatherless child was as valuable as any child in the world – and that 'of such is the kingdom of heaven'. We had a party, I remember, in the large end room of the vicarage, to proclaim that fact.

I mention that particular woman and her homeless baby because that baptism challenged me to do something about housing. I knew I couldn't proclaim the value of that child to God and do nothing about its housing. In due course, I became chairman of a London Council of Social Service Housing Committee, because of that woman and her baby and others in the parish like her. I formed a study group of ex-Cambridge students, on 'Housing', and we became trouble-some to the Housing Ministers of the day, Henry Brooke and Keith Joseph.

To put it another way: Baptism taught me about housing and politics: the politics of housing. It wasn't enough to bap-tize with water and leave that child homeless in Newington Lodge. And, of course, it's not only housing of which baptism speaks. If you say: 'Baptism is the proclamation that this child is a child of mine' you are soon into the subject of upbringing, and education, and schools, and hospitals, and quite a lot of other subjects.

I had a Christmas card, only this week, from a couple whose baby I baptized in hospital. The baby was born at a weekend. The hospital was probably understaffed. At any rate, since that weekend the hospital has admitted its responsi-bility for the brain damage to the child. Her whole life – and the life of her parents – has been terribly altered by that birth in hospital.

Yet baptism in the hospital to which the baby was trans-ferred was one of the most memorable occasions in all my ministry. It was important to proclaim that this brain-damaged little baby is a child of God.

It's not in the name of a kind of 'Adonis' Christ – a perfectly formed Christ – that we baptize, but in the name of someone who, as Isaiah said: 'In all our afflictions, he was afflicted.' The signing of the child with the sign of the cross is no empty ritual. It says that at some stage this infant may be – probably will be – confronted by the problem of suffering, and evil, and, indeed, mortality. We sign the child with the sign of the cross 'In token' – as the hymn says – 'that thou too shalt tread the path he travelled by.'

The last baptism I want to talk to you about this morning has not yet taken place. John, the father, was Secretary to the Archbishop's Commission on Urban Priority Areas called 'Faith in the City', with which I served. I got to know John as a friend, travelling with him from city to city. I conducted the blessing of his second marriage, to Ruth, two years ago; but John, this last year, working out in East Europe, caught a strange virus which went first to his heart and then to his brain, and I buried him only a few months ago. What John did not know was that Ruth was pregnant when he died. What Ruth did not know when John died was that she was pregnant with twins. The twins were born last week – Katie and Lucia. Alas, Lucia had been dead in the womb for several weeks.

Ruth was bereaved now of John and of one of the babies, but she still has Katie to love and look after. She asked me some very difficult questions, not least about how to care for the dead body of Lucia. I remembered that in some parts of the early church baptism was delayed until people were dying, and even until they were dead. I wondered whether Lucia and Katie should be baptized together. It would have been one way of proclaiming to the world, of both babies, 'This child is a child of mine.' In the end we decided Lucia should have a 'normal' funeral and Katie will have a 'normal' baptism.

It's appropriate – to say the least – that we should be thinking together about baptism eleven days before Christmas. We shall be thinking of *that* baby soon – the baby Jesus – and the child he became – and the man. As the carol says: 'Soon comes the cross, the nails, the piercing . . .'

Baby or grown man, it's still possible to say of Jesus and his baptism: 'Baptism is the proclamation by God that this child is a child of mine.' That he remained, all the thirty-three years of his life – whatever happened to him. Wherever he was. Whatever he got up to. And the same is true of us. 'Baptism is

the proclamation by God that this child is a child of mine.'
That's true of you – and me – as well as of any child or god-
child of ours.

Bibliography

Of books and works cited

Bailey, Simon, *The Well Within*, Darton, Longman and Todd 1996

Bell, G. K. A. (ed), *The War and the Kingdom of God*, Longmans 1915

— *The Kingship of Christ*, Penguin 1954

Bickersteth, John (ed), *The Bickersteth Diaries 1914–1918*, Pen and Sword Books 1996

Blake, William, *The Complete Poems*, Penguin 1977

Bonham-Carter, Mark and Pottle, Mark (eds), *Lantern Slides: The Diaries and Letters of Violet Bonham-Carter 1904–14*, Weidenfeld and Nicolson 1996

Clifford, James L., *Biography as an Art*, OUP 1962

Dictionary of National Biography, The, OUP 1988–89

Eliot, T. S., *Collected Poems 1909–62*, Faber 1974

Fletcher, Charles M., *Communication in Medicine*, Nuffield Provincial Hospitals Trust 1973

Forster, John, *The Life of Charles Dickens* ed J. W. Ley, Doubleday Doran 1928

Fort, Gertrud von le, *The Song at the Scaffold*, Sheed and Ward 1953

Fromm, Erich, *Fear of Freedom*, Routledge 1991

Holman, Bob, *Children and Crime*, Lion 1995

James, Eric, *The Double Cure*, Hodder 1957

— (ed), *Spirituality for Today* (contains the paper by Alan Ecclestone 'On Praying'), SCM Press 1967

— *A Life of Bishop John A.T. Robinson*, Collins 1987

Johnson, Edgar, *Charles Dickens*, Gollancz 1953

Julian of Norwich, *Revelations of Divine Love* ed Dom Roger Huddleston, Burns Oates 1927

Lilje, Hans, *The Last Book of the Bible*, Muhlenberg Press, Philadelphia 1957

Luckett Richard, *Handel's Messiah: A Celebration*, Gollancz 1992

Macdonald, George, *Poetical Works*, Macmillan 1893

Macquarrie, John and Childress, James, *A New Dictionary of Christian Ethics*, SCM Press 1986

O'Connor, OP, Jerome Murphy-, *The Theology of the Second Letter to the Corinthians*, CUP 1992

Oxford Study Bible, The, OUP 1992

Rifkin, Jeremy, *The End of Work*, Putnam 1995

Rhymes, Douglas, *No New Morality*, Constable 1964

— *Prayer in the Secular City*, Lutterworth 1967

— *Time Past to Time Future*, Darton, Longman and Todd 1993

Robinson, John A. T., 'The House Church and the Parish Church', *Theology*, August 1950

— *On Being the Church in the World*, SCM Press 1960

— *Honest to God*, SCM Press 1963

— *Exploration into God*, SCM Press 1967

— *The Human Face of God*, SCM Press 1973

— *Where Three Ways Meet: Last Essays and Sermons* (contains the sermon 'Learning from Cancer'), SCM Press 1987

Streeter, B. H. (ed), *Foundations. A Statement of Christian Belief in Terms of Modern Thought: by Seven Oxford Men*, Macmillan 1912

Thomas, Antony, *Rhodes: The Race for Africa*, BBC Books 1996

Thomas, R. S., *Collected Poems*, Dent 1993; Phoenix 1995

Toland, John, *Adolf Hitler*, Doubleday 1976

Toynbee, Arnold, *The Study of History*, OUP 1934–61

Updike, John, *In the Beauty of the Lilies*, Hamish Hamilton 1996

Vidler, A. D. (ed), *Soundings*, CUP 1962

Wakefield, Gordon S. (ed), *A Dictionary of Christian Spirituality*, SCM Press 1983

Warren, Max, *The Truth of Vision*, Canterbury Press 1948

Zeller, Eberhard, *The Flame of Freedom: The German Struggle against Hitler*, Westview Press 1994

Acknowledgments

The author and publishers are grateful to the following
for permission to quote from copyright work

Darton, Longman and Todd for extracts from Douglas Rhymes, *Time Past to Time Future*, 1993 and Simon Bailey, *The Well Within*, 1996

Faber and Faber for lines from T. S. Eliot, *Little Gidding* and *Choruses from 'The Rock'* in *Collected Poems 1909–62*, 1974

Hamish Hamilton for extracts from John Updike, *In the Beauty of the Lilies*, 1996

Orion Publishing Group for two poems by R. S. Thomas from his *Collected Poems 1945–1990*, Dent 1993

Oxford University Press for extracts from the *Dictionary of National Biography*, 1988–89; and for two hymns by Jan Struther from *Enlarged Songs of Praise*

Pen and Sword Books for extracts from John Bickersteth (ed), *The Bickersteth Diaries 1914–1918*, 1996

Weidenfeld and Nicolson for extracts from Mark Bonham-Carter and Mark Pottle (eds), *Lantern Slides: The Diaries and Letters of Violet Bonham-Carter 1904–14*, 1996